Along an African Border

CONTEMPORARY ETHNOGRAPHY

Kirin Narayan, Series Editor

A complete list of books
in the series is available from the publisher.

Along an African Border

Angolan Refugees and Their Divination Baskets

Sónia Silva

PENN

UNIVERSITY OF PENNSYLVANIA PRESS

PHILADELPHIA

Published by
University of Pennsylvania Press
Philadelphia, Pennsylvania 19104-4112
www.upenn.edu/pennpress

Printed in the United States of America
on acid-free paper

10 9 8 7 6 5 4 3 2 1

Library of Congress Cataloging-in-Publication Data
Silva, Sónia.
    Along an African border : Angolan refugees and their divination baskets / Sónia
Silva.
        p. cm. — (Contemporary ethnography)
    Includes bibliographical references and index.
    ISBN 978-0-8122-4293-5 (hardcover : alk. paper)
    1. Luvale (African people)—Zambia—Chavuma District—Rites and ceremonies.
2. Divination—Zambia—Chavuma District. 3. Baskets—Religious aspects—
Zambia—Chavuma District. 4. Fetishes (Ceremonial objects)—Zambia—Chavuma
District. 5. Chavuma District (Zambia)—Social life and customs. I. Title.
DT3058.L89S45   2011
299.6'8397—dc22   2010028056

To Keith and Julian

Life can only be understood backwards; but it must be lived forwards.

—Kierkegaard

Contents

1. Sakutemba's *lipele* (Chavuma, 1999; photo by author)

Western Zambia, Eastern Angola, and Southern Democratic Republic of the Congo

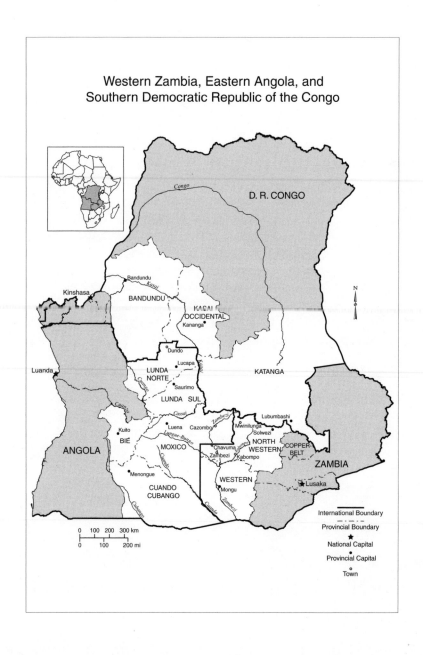

D. R. CONGO

Congo

Kinshasa

Bandundu

BANDUNDU

Kasai

KASAI OCCIDENTAL

Kananga

Dundo

Luanda

Lucapa

LUNDA NORTE

Saurimo

Kasai

KATANGA

LUNDA SUL

Cuango

Cuanza

Cassai

Lubumbashi

Luena Cazombo Mwinilunga

Zambezi

Solwezi

Kuito

Langue-Bungo

NORTH WESTERN

COPPER-BELT

BIÉ

MOXICO

Chavuma

Zambezi Kabompo

ANGOLA

Cuando

Zambezi

ZAMBIA

Menongue

WESTERN

Lusaka

CUANDO CUBANGO

Mongu

Cubango

Zambezi

N

International Boundary
Provincial Boundary
★ National Capital
● Provincial Capital
○ Town

0 100 200 300 km
0   100   200 mi

Introduction

A *lipele* is a basket that contains sixty or so small articles, from seeds, claws, and minuscule horns to coins and wooden carvings. These articles have individual names and symbolic meanings; collectively, they are known as *jipelo*.[1] People in northwest Zambia will tell you that a *lipele* is first and foremost a material object, a *chuma*, much like a food basket, a hammer, a stool, or a house. Yet they will also say that the *lipele* is an extraordinary object. A *lipele*, it is said, is capable of thinking, hearing, judging, and responding; it communicates by means of *jipelo* articles drawn in configurations, punishes wrongdoers, assists people in need, and, much like humans, goes through a life course. This is not to suggest that the *lipele* is seen as a human person and self, a *mutu*. In my two years of fieldwork in Chavuma, a district of northwest Zambia located along the Angolan border, no one showed interest in such ontological quandaries, but it took little time and research to realize that the *lipele* lacks at least one basic human attribute: a human body (*mujimba wamutu*). What, then, is the *lipele*? What kind of entity is this, which is and is not a thing and is and is not a person?

The Fetish in "Fetish"

The idea of *fetish* comes to mind, but the term is loaded with prejudice. *Fetish* derives from *fetisso*, a Pidgin word that emerged in the mercantile, multicultural context of the Guinea Coast in the sixteenth and seventeenth centuries (Pietz 1985, 1987, 1988). In the words of William Smith, an Englishman who embarked on a voyage to Guinea in 1726, "fittish" refers to "some Trifle or other, to which they [Pagans] pay a particular Respect, or Kind of Adoration, believing it can defend them from all Danger's: Some have a Lion's Tail; some a Bird's Feather. Some a Pebble, a Bit of Rag, a Dog's Leg; or, in short, any thing they fancy" (1744:26, quoted in Pietz 1987:41). In the eyes of Smith and other Europeans who traveled to Guinea, many of them merchants, *fetissos* stood for Africans, people who live in chaos and lack reason, adoring any thing they fancy

2. An Angolan diviner at work (Museu Nacional de Etnologia, Portugal; photo by Benjamin Pereira in Dundo, Angola, 1971)

and failing to distinguish between objects and humans. In 1757, Charles de Brosses would turn *fetishes* into *fetishism*, a discourse of otherness into a primitive mode of thought, and it was through the work of de Brosses that *fetishes* came to influence nineteenth- and early twentieth-century thinkers, such as Comte, Marx, and Freud (Ellen 1988).

As early as the late nineteenth century, however, the concept of *fetish* came under attack. In 1884, William Robertson-Smith dismissed it as "a merely popular term which conveys no precise idea, but is vaguely supposed to mean something very savage and contemptible" (1884:209, quoted in Ellen 1988:215). In 1906, Marcel Mauss denounced the "unmerited and fortuitous role that the notion of *fetish* has played in theoretical and descriptive works," because "it corresponds to nothing but an immense misunderstanding between two civilizations, the African and the European" (1968:112, quoted in Pietz 1993:133). More recently, William Pietz has shown that fetishism, far from being specific to a concrete society or type of societies, is a "problem-idea" of Enlightenment theory whose pedigree he meticulously traces back, as mentioned, to the sixteenth- and seventeenth-century cross-cultural region of West Africa (1985).

One would think that the term *fetish* would have become anathema in anthropology and been dismissed as vague, useless, depreciative, and racist. One would think that it would have been at the very least conceptually reconstituted as a historical misunderstanding between two civilizations, as Pietz proposes. Maybe it is a testament to the fetishistic qualities of the term itself that anthropologists continue to surrender to its enchantment. There is no other term like it—*ritual object*, *sacred object*, or *power figure* can hardly compare with *fetish*—so anthropologists and other scholars continue using it, while at the same time they strive in all earnestness to separate themselves from its tainted history. Thus it is that the embarrassment of a historically loaded and loathsome term has given way to the embarrassment of an apologetic expression: "*fetish* in quotes."

Most anthropologists today, though, are no longer using fetishism as a discourse of difference. Not only are they recognizing that divination baskets and other such entities are as active as ever throughout the world, from Zambia to Europe, but also they are using fetishism as a discourse of sameness.

Consider Wyatt MacGaffey's fascinating study of *minkisi*, those visually striking figurines, clay pots, gourds, bundles, and other containers from the early twentieth-century Lower Congo with empowering spirits that come from the land of the dead (2000). Best known to the world is a subclass of these, the awe-inspiring *nkondi*, often prized in ethnographic and art museums as "nail fetishes." Although MacGaffey reminds his readers that the *minkisi* ought to be understood in their original sociocultural and historical context, he also recognizes basic functional similarities between them and a spate of Western objects, religious and secular: relics of saints in medieval Europe, national monuments, engagement rings, national flags, and works of art (1990). At least functionally, MacGaffey appears to be suggesting that we are all fetishists, if not literally, then with quotes.

Roy Ellen arrives at the same conclusion from a different theoretical perspective. Having studied fetishism among the Nualu of Seram, Indonesia, he offers good reasons to accept its universality on cognitive grounds and, consequently, to use the term without quotes—even though, he tells us, he has "no particular desire to salvage terms once thought obsolete or retain old concepts as they stand, and thinks [that he] would actually resist applying the word 'fetish' to ritual objects [he] might encounter in the course of ethnographic analysis" (1988:232, 1990). The label may be irremediably tarnished, but Ellen assures us that there are fetishes and there is fetishism. Nualu sacred shields, Kongo *minkisi*, Bamana *boli*, Fon *bocio*, Luvale *lipele*, and other such entities studied in anthropology and art history are well-known examples of fetishes; other examples are the hands, feet, buttocks, fur, safety pins, high-heeled shoes, items of female underclothing, and other nongenital objects and parts of anatomy of mostly Western, male pathological obsession, studied in psychology, and the equally mystifying commodity fetishes of capitalism, studied by Marx. All fetishes, Western and non-Western, are created through the same cognitive processes: concretization (objectification of a concept), animation, conflation of signifier and signified, and development of an ambiguous relationship of control between object and person (Ellen 1988). Where MacGaffey sees function, Ellen sees cognition.[2]

There is a third, more radical alternative: drop the term entirely and study the phenomenon from a perspective that is ideologically less problematic and heuristically more inclusive—commoditization. For Arjun Appadurai and Igor Kopytoff, all things everywhere make new sense in the light of this perspective, be it Korean toothpicks, slaves on the Middle Passage, oriental carpets, relics of saints from early medieval Europe, funerary canoes from the Solomon Islands, Lozi royal property, designer-label clothing, human fetuses, or Turkmen saddlebags. Appadurai and Kopytoff are interested in the exchangeability potential of all things regardless of what kind of thing they are, and they claim that it is possible to trace their movement in and out of the commodity state by following what Kopytoff calls their "cultural biography" (1986). And, in the same way that persons come to realize their personhood potential by different means and to different degrees, so do things realize their exchangeability potential differently, some remaining in the commodity state from beginning to end and others being removed permanently or temporarily from that state and placed elsewhere—the case of the *lipele*. Lest we forget the commodity potential of all things, even the most singular and sacred, Appadurai labels the latter "ex-commodities" or, because of the zeal with which they are protected and guarded from commoditization, "enclaved commodities" (1986a:16, 22-23).

Notwithstanding their theoretical differences, all these authors (MacGaffey, Ellen, Appadurai, and Kopytoff) stand on common ground. They all see the ambiguity between thingness and personhood as the defining characteristic of fetishism. However phrased to suit particular approaches—person and object or singularity and commodity—ontological categories are seen as fluid. MacGaffey perceives a continuum between the personification of *minkisi* and the objectification of Kongo chiefs in Bakongo political culture (1988:203, 2000:135). Appadurai (1986a) and Kopytoff (1986) speak of "commoditization" instead of "commodities" and expand their model to dialectically encompass both the commoditization of persons and singularization of things. And Ellen's cognitive approach contemplates the ambiguous power relation between fetish and fetishist (1988:228-29). Once erroneously taken by Auguste Comte and other Enlightenment intellectuals for a sign of malthought, deluded causality, and inferiority, ontological ambiguity is now seen as universal, dynamic, and creative.

Personification, Objectification, De-Objectification

I agree that ontological ambiguity is the crux of fetishism. From here on, however, I place in abeyance the question of which continuum—personification, fetishization, or (de)commoditization—best captures the biography of the *lipele*, a question that is dangerously close to searching for its true value—social, cognitive, or economic—and asking what kind of thing it is—person, fetish, or commodity. I also avoid as much as possible the kindred vocabulary in my ethnographic descriptions and, in a phenomenological spirit, move to historically situated social perception and existential concerns. For the men and women whom I met in Chavuma in the mid-1990s, what the *lipele* *is* hardly raises any interest, even for diviners (*vakakutaha*). For them, the *lipele is* what the *lipele does,* and because what the *lipele* does is divining, the *lipele* is an oracle (*ngombo*). "Oracles" is the class of objects in which the *lipele* rightly belongs, next to medicated pestles, mortars, bottles, mirrors, and human figures.

Furthermore, because divining is by definition an intersubjective practice (divination is always performed for someone else—and this someone is, existentially speaking, objectified), I suggest that the personification of an object is not only entailed with the diviner's controlled objectification through spirit possession within the bounded space of ritual but also with the engaged, passionate attempt by the diviner and his clients to de-objectify themselves outside ritual. The personification of a material object is ultimately devoid of meaning if severed from the existential objectification and de-objectification of individual subjects. The value of the *lipele*, in addition to being social, cognitive, and economic, is necessarily intersubjective and existential.

Note that by *objectification* I mean the sense of existential powerlessness, uncertainty, and diminution—the sense, to invert Grace Harris's definition of personhood, of having no standing (not "status") in a social order, of
being a "nobody" incapable of acting or whose actions are of no consequence
(1989:602). Although the sense of powerlessness that accompanies, say, a debilitating disease or childlessness in adulthood is often elusive (Silva 2009), in
other cases, such as slavery and spirit possession, it may crystallize in cultural
and social practice or become somatized. Psychological trauma may lead to the
experience of paralysis, immobilization, withdrawal, automatization, or roboti-
zation.[3] Persons interact with one another in a social world, and these interac-
tions are as likely to become constructive as to become destructive. Being a
person always entails the possibility of being nullified, ignored by others, forgotten, crushed, discarded, brushed off, kicked around, or blown up. In health
or in illness the risk of becoming an object is ever present. "In no human society it is possible to draw anything but a transient and ambiguous line between
subject and object," says anthropologist Michael Jackson. "In our practical
lives, the line is infringed continually. The field of intersubjectivity inescapably
involves an ongoing reciprocal movement in consciousness between a sense of
being a subject for oneself and being an object for others" (1998:77).

Basket divination is one way objectified individuals attempt to de-objectify
themselves. How is the process of de-objectification perceived and achieved?
To answer this question we must bear in mind that basket divination is a way
of coping with adversity. Let us now consider three important ways in which
divination was understood in northwest Zambia at the time of my fieldwork:
a way of doing, a way of knowing, and a way of making a living.

Three Facets

Basket divination as a *way of doing* is ritual efficacy; it is doing things through
ritual. In this book, I reveal how divinatory rituals do what they are supposed
to do, paying close attention to ritual action, symbolism, and performative skill.
With David Parkin (1991) and Richard Werbner (1989), I give equal importance to the interaction between ritual participants and the performative role
of discourse; with Filip de Boeck and René Devisch (1994), I focus on symbolism. Although basket divination, as de Boeck and Devisch argue, is a "happening" that produces itself independently of the participants' personal motives
and the consequences it has on their society, it remains ultimately dependent
on their skilled participation in the performance. I draw on the work of these

authors—and on Victor Turner on liminality (1967, 1982) and Stanley Tambiah on ritual efficacy (1968, 1979)—to show that *lipele* rituals can produce results only if key symbols and performative elements are used with skill.

Basket divination, however, is much more than ritual form and performance. When a consulting party (*vatewa*) approaches a *lipele*, its members and the relative they represent find themselves in a critical state of obscurity and indecision. They hope that the revelation of knowledge will bring clarity, lead to spiritually sanctioned action, and bring some measure of control over life and events. Basket divination is a way of unraveling the cause of past and present troubles; it is a *way of knowing*.

Rescuing Africans from the miry realm of belief, which in the history of anthropology and Western philosophical thought is vaguely defined in opposition to so-called true knowledge, several authors have given analytical priority to this search for knowledge and depicted African divination (African traditional thought in general) as an epistemological system akin to Western science. This line of reasoning, however, leads to difficulties. For Robin Horton, African traditional thought constitutes a scientific but "closed" predicament, the awareness of alternatives being remarkably less developed than in the Western "open" predicament (1993/1967:153). For Igor Kopytoff, the Suku of the Democratic Republic of the Congo *know* (do not simply believe) that their ancestors exist, their system of thought being comparable to science, but this science of theirs differs from ours, corresponding to the nineteenth-century ideal of Positivism (1981). And, for Michael Jackson, the Kuranko pebble divinatory technique used in Sierra Leone is akin to social science, but its outlook is Positivist, because both systems use arcane vocabularies, a depersonalized style, and ceremonial forms of denying subjectivity; like the Positivist, the Kuranko diviner is "allegedly passive and receptive, the technique allegedly objective, the procedure allegedly impersonal" (1989:56). With one stroke, these authors promote African religious thought to a coeval epistemology and denigrate it to an anachronistic endeavor, if not a bastard science, as Frazer had once said of magic.

Jackson, however, soon veers onto a different route. Having placed Kuranko divination and Western science on the same footing, he refocuses his analysis under a pragmatist and existentialist light. The Kuranko as consulters, it turns out, have no interest in abstract questions of veracity because they view divinatory knowledge instrumentally (1996:6, 13).[4] I see *lipele* knowledge in the same light. For the Luvale and related peoples, as for the Kuranko, divinatory knowledge is wedded to the pressing needs of daily life.

For them, basket divination is not an epistemological exercise; it is a way of knowing that facilitates action.

I also circumvent the knowledge-belief dichotomy by depicting divination as embodied knowledge, a form of knowing in which there are no propositions to be true or false. To portray divination as an epistemology is to refer to propositional knowledge—Gilbert Ryle's "knowledge that" as distinct from "knowledge how" (1949:25-61)—the only type of knowledge that overlaps with belief. As Anthony Quinton points out, "Belief is always propositional or believing that; there is no believing how that serves as a defective version of knowing how to do something" (1967:346). Although it would be incorrect to disregard the importance of propositional knowledge in *lipele* divination, as we will see in Chapter 3, embodied knowledge is at least as fundamental. Not only is embodied knowledge of great significance in a political context where the re-articulation of one's identity, as will be shortly explained, cannot be achieved through narration (knowing-how is also remembering-how), embodied knowledge is also consistent with the definition of basket divination as a performative, practical activity.

And this brings me to the diviners' understanding of their profession as a *way of making a living*. Epistemological approaches compare divination to science, and symbolist and performative approaches compare it to theater and the arts. Devisch, for example, sees divination as an "artistic creation," a "happening," a play in which the actor is the play's own "autodialectical production," an agglomerate of "forms, colors, rhythms, volumes interacting and embracing one another, rather than . . . fulfilling . . . the project of the artist or his patron or the spectator" (1985:71; see also Beattie 1964:61, 1966). Although these metaphors capture very vividly the expressive quality of divinatory rituals, they have the unfortunate effect of understating the reason why they are conducted in the first place. In the West, art is often created, performed, and judged independently of the anxieties and preoccupations of both artists and art viewers; a *lipele* session, however, is always conducted for someone in need.

Begging the question some, I should mention here how basket divination was described to me. No allusion was ever made to theater, art, or science. Laypeople who were potential consulters portrayed it as a quest for knowledge, a quest that is given metaphorical expression in the definition of each séance as a journey toward clarity (see Chapter 3). The diviners spoke of their rituals as a means to earn a livelihood, as they would of farming, fishing, and hunting. And by perceiving rituals, which they saw as qualitatively different from secular activities, as nonetheless secular, they urged me to dispense with such dichotomies as theory versus common sense, expressive versus instrumental, and sacred versus profane (Tambiah 1990).

There is an important difference between understanding basket divination as a way of knowing and as a way of making a living: the first appears to be universal and constitutive of divination as a cultural practice; the second is a reflection of the dire living conditions in 1990s Chavuma. This difference, however, should not conceal an equally important similarity: the existential equivalence between the consulters' suffering and the diviners' suffering. In the end, consulters and diviners are both sufferers for whom basket divination brings a measure of control over life and events.

The Experience of Adversity

I was often told that Chavuma, named by the Luvale chief Sakutemba Kaweshi after the rumbling waterfalls in the Zambezi River (*Chavuma* derives from *kuvuma*, "to rumble") had once been a land of abundant resources. Once the Zambezi and Kashiji rivers had overflowed with fish, the forests had swelled with game, the pale, windblown Kalahari sands that constitute the surface soil had been rich and fertile. Chavuma was no longer what it had once been, and the ones to blame, I was told, were the increasing numbers of Angolan refugees.

The first noticeable influx of Angolans occurred in the 1920s and 1930s. The Portuguese had recently established military posts in the eastern border region of Angola, and, by the 1920s, they were collecting taxes and recruiting unpaid *corvée* labor (Clarence-Smith 1983:186-87, Newitt 2008:45-60). To escape these burdens or seek employment in the mines of Northern Rhodesia (now Zambia), Belgian Congo (now the Democratic Republic of the Congo), or South Africa, many villagers chose to cross the international borders. Between 1940 and 1950, the population of the border regions of Angola declined by 16 to 22 percent (Newitt 2008:64).[5]

Discontent grew in the colony, and, in the 1960s, Angolans rebelled. A string of insurrections broke out in the north, central highlands, and Luanda, leading rapidly to military operations spearheaded by nationalist movements. Until 1966, most conflicts occurred in the northern region, with the guerrillas operating out of Zaire (now the Democratic Republic of the Congo). In 1966, however, a new front was opened in the east, as two separate liberation movements, the MPLA (Popular Movement for the Liberation of Angola) and UNITA (National Union for the Total Independence of Angola), set up military bases in newly independent Zambia. Caught in the middle, accused of treason by both sides, villagers were resettled to colonial townships by the Portuguese and terrorized by the guerrillas. Several of the individuals mentioned in this book, including the basket diviners, arrived in Zambia at this time.

Independence came in 1975, after thirteen years of military conflict. The thrill of freedom, however, did not last. In the run for political power in independent Angola, the opposing liberation movements forged alliances with the Cold War superpowers. The MPLA turned to Cuba and the USSR, and UNITA reached out to apartheid South Africa and the United States, thus locking the country in what David Birmingham calls "a war by proxy between the United States and the Soviet Union" (2006:111). The FNLA (National Front for the Liberation of Angola), a third nationalist movement, was defeated in combat by the MPLA in 1975. The Cold War ended in the early 1990s, but the Angolan civil war continued, as the MPLA and UNITA found new ways to fund their military operations with national natural resources, the MPLA with oil and UNITA with diamonds.[6]

By the end of 2001, just a few months prior to the cease-fire in April 2002, about 210,000 Angolans were living in Zambia (USCR 2002:53, UNHCR 2002:5). Some resided willingly or unwillingly in the official refugee settlements of Mayukwayukwa and Meheba, others stayed in the villages and townships of Western and North-Western provinces, and others still reached as far as the cities of the Copperbelt and Lusaka.[7] In 1950, Chavuma's population was 3,003 (Hansen 1976:126); in 2000, following half a century of almost uninterrupted war, its population had grown seven times to a reported total of 21,617 (Central Statistical Office 2001).[8] These were times of suffering and deep discontent.

In the mid-1990s, at the time of my fieldwork, the roots of suffering were visible in the physical and social landscape. The area adjoining the thirteenth parallel south, which constitutes the northern border, looked as if a giant machete had stabbed the earth and pushed all the trees southward. Although the Angolan side was densely covered with a thicket of grown trees, the Zambian side had hardly any forest left, every acre of land having been cleared for cassava fields. It is true that fruit trees and sugarcane studded the villages (*membo*); that the Christian Missions in Many Lands (CMML), founded in 1923, still provided some opportunities for trade, employment, and the services of a hospital; and that the motor road linked Chavuma to the township of Zambezi and the cities of the Copperbelt, prohibitive as transportation costs were. Most important, there was no war in Chavuma. But, in the 1990s, this was all there was to celebrate. People complained that there was hardly any land left to cultivate, any forest to clear, any game to hunt, and any fish to trap in the rivers and flooded plains. Having once lived in sparsely populated areas with abundant natural resources, many Angolans were now obliged to purchase farmland and even fish and meat to eat, or, in the absence of cash, to eat leaf dishes day in and day out, feeling neither full nor satisfied.

Chavuma was also enveloped in silence. The 1970 Zambian Refugees Control Act states very clearly that all refugees must live in official camps. In the late 1960s and early 1970s, government officials directly instructed the villagers to report any "strangers" to the authorities (Hansen 1976:27-28). For these "strangers"—the Angolans illegally settled along the border, among their kin—this translated into fear of repatriation or resettlement to the Meheba Refugee Settlement, located near Solwezi. They became distrustful of everyone, relative, neighbor, or stranger. In the 1990s, the Zambian government was no longer seeking out illegal refugees who had arrived prior to 1985, as is the case of the diviners and many others mentioned in this book, and many refugees had obtained Zambian registration cards, thus becoming de jure citizens (Hansen 1990:7, USCR 1987:21). Still the Angolans lived in fear. Maybe they were no longer illegal refugees. Maybe they would no longer be resettled to Meheba. Maybe they should no longer fear *delatores*. Life, however, had taught them that everything could change in a moment. It had in the past, and it could again.

Silencing the past stemmed also from fear of the past and not only from fear of the present. Violated individuals may repress or deny their painful memories, lack words to describe atrocities that are beyond their moral and conceptual thresholds, or protect themselves from the past by keeping their memories at bay, neither quite forgetting nor quite remembering them. A young Zimbabwean told Werbner that freedom fighters "don't like to talk about the war and their fighting. They sometimes sit alone or with others not talking, and they don't want to tell others about their experiences, which grieve them and trouble their thoughts so much they just want to forget" (1991:157-58). To relive the past in reminiscence is to reenter it, not simply to represent it cognitively. Although the events and experiences lived in Angola could never be forgotten, they could at least be set aside by filling the days with chores and harmless chatter. The Angolans strove to fence off their lives in the present, away from the tormenting memories of the past and the insecurity of the future. The silence about the past was a conspicuous presence in Chavuma, as real and consequential as the words said and the things touched. It was collective, and it attested to a shared past and a shared present.

It was in this context that I carried out fieldwork on the topic of basket divination. During my preliminary research trip to Chavuma in 1994, I had assumed that the presence of basket diviners in the area had to do with the end of British rule, which had declared witch hunting (and, therefore, basket divination) illegal, and perhaps with the area's relative remoteness as well. That presence, however, was more directly related to Chavuma's proximity to Angola, a country where change had been abrupt and catastrophic. The diviners and many of their clients were Angolan refugees.

And yet, I could not identify any significant difference between basket divination in wartime and basket divination in peacetime. In the process of transmuting particular experiences of suffering into structural nodes of relationship and prototypical emotions, basket divination omitted recent history. The new and contingent fused with the old and universal.

The divination case described in Chapter 3 illustrates this process of fusion. A small boy was suffering from epilepsy, and the diviner consulted attributed the failure to cure him to a matrilineal ancestor who had accidentally shot himself while hunting for game in the bush. This ancestor, the diviner said, had afflicted the boy because some of his descendants, all Angolans, had shamelessly accused each other of being slaves. For both the diviner and the boy's father, who took the case for divining, the Angolan identity of the boy's relatives and the mentioning of slavery, both historical phenomena, were surely no mere trivialities; their priority, however, was to identify the affliction (the ancestor's accidental death) and its ultimate origin (the dissent and disrespect among relatives) because these rather customary phenomena were the ones that had to be addressed by ritual and therapeutic means if the boy was to recover. The ravages of the Angolan war and the politics of resettlement in Zambia were certainly real, well-known to all, and overpowering, but they did not change in any significant way the operational scope of basket divination, including the kind of predicaments considered, the divinatory procedure, the diagnoses offered, and the remedial measures prescribed.

This had not always been the case. During colonialism, the Luvale etiological pantheon had expanded considerably to include new kinds of afflicting agents and afflictions, all of which became represented in divination baskets. Some of these agents and afflictions, referred to by the same name—*sitima* (train), *ndeke* (plane), and *vindele* (Europeans)—were said to derive from contact with things non-African, from imported motorized vehicles in urban areas to Europeans. According to Charles White, a British colonial officer and an anthropologist, the curative ritual for *vindele* was "partially carried in a house in which articles of European material culture [had] been placed and the ritual meal [consisted] of Portuguese dishes such as fowl with rice, tomatoes and onions, and beer served in a bottle and drunk from a glass" (1961:50).[9] A careful look at the *jipelo* articles will also reveal material traces of previous historical periods, suggesting that basket divination is a way of remembering the past (Blier 1995, Shaw 2002). Among the *jipelo* are coins dating from colonialism, cowrie shells transported from the Indian Ocean by Europeans, and even a wooden figure called Slave, Ndungo, which represents pre-colonial, African forms of slavery but exhibits chains or ropes around the neck, material representations of the Atlantic slave trade.

In 1990s Chavuma, however, the *lipele* baskets had no *jipelo* that bespoke directly or indirectly of contemporary politics. There were no material representations of war victims, war perpetrators, or war refugees; no new additions to the etiological pantheon; and no verbal acknowledgment of the Angolan wars, forced displacement, or even the country of Angola in direct relation to the consulters' predicaments.[10] In anthropology, material oracles have been described as microcosms of social life and, more recently, as repositories of social emotions and experiences (Graw 2009:105). Although we know that basket divination symbols are multireferential, their referents being highly autonomous and disclosing different truths new or old in different configurations (Turner 1975/1961:221), it is still perplexing, if not perturbing, that in the 1990s divination baskets lacked any material representation of things Angolan.

Maybe the Angolans sought in basket divination what they lacked in life—continuity. The value of cultural continuity is likely to increase proportionally to the level of social violence, and, in the 1990s, social violence in the border region had skyrocketed. Or maybe basket divination was an accomplice in the local environment of silence and fear, the experiences and emotions associated with Angola and life in exile being represented in the baskets not in the form of material objects but by the absence of material objects. Speaking of the Sakalava of Madagascar, Michael Lambek discusses the silencing of stories about spirits whose lives were associated with excessive acts of violence. "The sign of the truth of the story," he argues, "is not its retelling but its silence or the punishment that accompanies narration. . . . The difficulty of speaking about the past is a salient index of its significance" (1998:123). So is the difficulty of speaking about the present.

How, then, does one acknowledge change in the study of an activity that prioritizes continuity? My answer to this challenge is to situate the world of basket divination in its larger social, political, and historical context because such is the context in which the diviners, consulters, and I all met and in which they lived their lives. At the same time, however, much like the diviners, I prioritize basket divination as a way of dealing with the mundane miseries that divination has always helped people cope with: illness, reproductive problems, sexual impotence, and death. In the 1990s, suffering and adversity took many forms. My concern, however, is not to study these forms according to their cause, old or new, and much less their intensity, high or low, but to consider suffering through the lens of basket divination.[11]

Narrative Threads

To convey the fluidity of personhood and thingness as they traverse physical boundaries (people and things) and realms of practice (ritual and secular), I have interwoven this book with two narrative threads: with one thread I draw on the narrative framework of field notes written during fieldwork to describe my experiences and process of data collection. Inspired by Kopytoff's biographical approach to things, I devoted part of my fieldwork to accompanying several divination baskets as they were born, as they became initiated, and as they died. It is this methodology, and the things and people it led me to, that this narrative thread describes.

I had originally intended to apprentice myself to a diviner. I wanted to learn by doing (rather than learning exclusively by tracing the biography of things, observing, and interviewing). The diviners, however, politely but firmly declined my request. Basket diviners are always men whose initiation into divination is forced on them by their ancestors. As a foreigner, I may have been perceived as gender-ambiguous and been taught valuable knowledge that no diviner would ever share with a local woman, but I was definitely not seen as a man. Neither was I perceived as a full member of their society, despite my adoption by two *manduna* headmen, *nduna* Maseka and *nduna* Mutonga, and christening with a Luvale name, Sombo. Diviners were willing to share some of their knowledge with me and allow me to attend some of their rituals, but formal apprenticeship was impossible.

For this reason, I had to rely more heavily than I had anticipated and wished on the classic methodological cycle: (1) observation of events, (2) recorded interviewing about those events, (3) transcription of interviews, (4) reading and interpretation of the transcribed interviews, and (5) further interviewing. I am very grateful to Henry Sawendele for his meticulous work of transcribing my tape-recorded interviews, and to the late Roy Mbundu and Cedric Chikunga for their research assistance. Without them, it would have been impossible to overcome the initial suspicion that stiffened all meetings and to carry out conversations on esoteric topics that proved daunting to my moderate fluency in the Luvale language. Together, sometimes in the Luvale language and other times by translation into English, we learned much about basket divination. As I traced the cultural biography of particular baskets, as mentioned earlier, I came to know some diviners better than others. I am deeply thankful to Sangombe, Sakutemba, Sanjamba, and Mutondo.

Most events described in this book took place between February and December 1996. I had arrived in Chavuma in May 1995, but it took time and perseverance to learn Luvale, a West Central Bantu language, familiarize myself with the highly esoteric world of basket divination, and receive permission to record rituals. The ritual of delivering the basket, which I describe in Chapter 1, and the ritual that initiates the new basket into a mature oracle, which I describe in Chapter 2, are only rarely performed. Neither has ever been documented.

In addition to the limitations imposed by language, social identity, and esoterism, I faced other challenges during my fieldwork. My relationship with diviners was inescapably affected by the political and economic realities already in place: international refugee law and the world's political and economic asymmetries. I was a young female from Portugal, the European country that had colonized Angola, and I had been living in the United States. All in all, I was simply another *chindele,* a white foreigner who had arrived uninvited, a threat to their safety and cultural entitlement. Other foreigners had been after their commodities; I was after their tradition (*chisemwa*).

A daughter of militant parents who in their youth had fought in Portugal to overthrow the dictatorship that had held Angola for so long, I could hardly identify with the ghastly image of the colonizer or the diamond smuggler. But I accepted the Angolans' standpoint and took up the burden of "my" history. I also accepted the limits of my fieldwork.

With my first narrative thread, I describe my fieldwork process and experiences; with my second, I trace my intellectual trajectory and discovery from the time of fieldwork to the time of writing. In the mid-1990s, I had left for Zambia determined to unveil how anthropomorphization (the continuum subject-object) played out in the specific sociocultural and historical context of Chavuma. I had planned to follow the cultural biography of divination baskets, a methodology that seemed consistent with the idea that divination baskets, being personified, have lives of their own. I had also anticipated corroborating commoditization theory, a theory that resonated well with my interest in fluidity (the opposite of the Positivist fixation on natural kinds) and provided me with both a method of data collection and a conceptual kit. Appadurai and Kopytoff had changed the study of material culture in the late 1980s, and I wanted to become a part of that historical turn.

Fieldwork showed me, however, that the strength of this theory is also its weakness. Commoditization theory hurried me along from village to village, it predisposed me to look backward to the origins of the *lipele* and forward to the future of the *lipele* and, in so doing, it disinclined me to pause, take a seat, observe, chat, and spend time with others. I struggled to mask my growing sense that commoditization theory overlooked the specificity of the *lipele* as a ritual entity and its historical and existential significance. In this book, I reconcile myself with my fieldwork experience and accept the analytical consequences of privileging life in its own right. In the same process, I also reconcile myself with the presence of Victor Turner in my work.

I confess that I never intended to restudy the sociocultural world that Turner encountered in Northern Rhodesia (now Zambia) in the mid-1950s— true though it is that the Luvale, Chokwe, Luchazi, and Mbunda who reside in Chavuma are closely related to the Ndembu of Mwinilunga District, studied by Turner. All these groups (as well as the Lunda-Shinde who are often called Southern Lunda, together with the Ndembu) share a matrilineal and virilocal social organization, a similar cultural complex best known for the boys' initiation ceremony, *mukanda*, and a common historical origin in Musumba, in what is now the southwestern corner of the Democratic Republic of the Congo.[12] Yet, both in the field and in writing, I often had the impression that I was conversing with Turner. His work on performance, liminality, ritual symbolism, color classification, rituals of affliction, and basket divination— most prominently in "Ndembu Divination: Its Symbolism and Techniques" (1975/1961) and "Muchona the Hornet, Interpreter of Religion" (1967/1959)— have inspired my thinking and writing in many ways. And although he came to refine his ideas in later years, it was in the Upper Zambezi, among the Ndembu, that they first blossomed.

With Turner in mind, who always intersected his interest in liminality with his interest in social dramas, I locate my book at the meeting point between ritual and everyday life. This is the point where the path of (de)commoditization leads to the liminal space of ritual, and the ritual-bound ontological continuum subject-object reaches over to everyday life, imbued with existential significance. Thingness and personhood are not essences arrested within the boundaries of different entities but endpoints of an ontological and existential continuum along which transient, contextualized expressions of objectification and personification arise. With MacGaffey, Kopytoff, and Appadurai, I suggest that we speak of processes—personification and objectification—instead of essences—persons and objects. Unlike them, however, I claim that such processes not only are inverted expressions of the same continuum but also are ontologically and existentially entangled. In other words, objectification and personification are intentionally activated in ritual so that objectified individuals attain de-objectification outside ritual. In 1990s Chavuma, this triangular continuum (personification of an object–objectification of a subject–and de-objectification of objectified subjects) became reflected in the social perception of basket divination as a way of doing, a way of knowing, and a way of making a living.

The risk of attributing reality to the methodologically justified pretense that a thing's significance lies in itself and not in social relationships—the risk of fetishizing what Appadurai calls "methodological fetishism" (1986a:5)—is ever present. Refusing to reduce the *lipele* to a mere reflection of the human mind, however defined, I show that the value of the personified object does not lie in itself but rather in contextual relation. Anthropomorphization is "relational and context-dependent, not classificatory and context free" (Gell 1998:22). Ontology goes hand in hand with intention, essence with appearance, reality with perception, and culture with history.

As a contribution to the study of divination systems and the continuum subject-object in the light of existential and historical contingencies, this book is a response to John Davis's cry to unite "the comfortable anthropology of social organization" to "the painful anthropology of disruption and despair" (1992:149). Today, the situation of the Angolan refugees in Zambia is no longer what it was prior to the end of the Angolan civil wars in 2002. Over 180,000 refugees have already returned to Angola, and it is estimated that by December 2011 there will be no more than 10,810 Angolan refugees remaining in Zambia (UNHCR 2009). I hope that this book testifies to the vitality and existential significance of an old cultural practice in the face of the catastrophic circumstances of the 1990s. Is not basket divination one way humanity was lived along the Angolan border?

1

Birth

I wished from the start to work closely with Sanjamba,[1] a senior diviner renowned for his wisdom, boldness, and wealth. He headed a populous and prosperous village; had several wives and many children; owned cattle and two big houses with glass windows; and among his smaller possessions he counted a sling reclining chair, a radio, a bicycle, and an oxcart newly painted in bright blue, reading on one side: *Kumona Njamba* (Seeing the elephant), a shorthand for the Luvale proverb *Kumona njamba kwenda* (Only he who travels sees the elephant). His praise name was Kufumana chaPawa Mwiza Kuchimbachila Ngimbu (The Fame of the Pawa Fruit Fools People to Carry an Axe) because he was as renowned and as likely to bewilder his visitors as the blue, shrub-growing *pawa* fruit, which, because of its fame, misleads people into thinking that it grows on a large tree. Aware of his might, Sanjamba rejoiced in displaying his practicing license as a registered diviner. It was not so much that this document ratified Sanjamba's Zambian identification card, which the Traditional Healers and Practitioners Association had used to determine his Zambian citizenship, important as this always is for a refugee; rather, his license represented the official recognition of a skill acquired in Angola and so integral a part of his identity.

As for working with Sanjamba, it never materialized. Again and again, research-bound, I would peddle thirteen kilometers of sandy terrain to Sanjamba's village in Chilyakawa, only to discover that Sanjamba was absent, wished to postpone the meeting, or could only talk for a short while. Sanjamba excelled at hiding information that later, on a whim, he offered freely. I had hoped to work closely with Sanjamba; in the end, however, the first person to draw my attention to the biography of the *lipele* was not even a diviner.

The Fisherman's Lesson

I first met Kakoma on 9 February 1996. Roy Mbundu, my first research assistant, and I had walked all the way to his village, hoping to meet his daughter Alice. She was known in the area as the skilled basket maker who in her childhood had fallen into an open fire. No sooner had we sat down to watch Alice coiling a flour basket than Kakoma picked up a stool and joined us beneath the mango tree. He introduced himself to us as the head-man (*chilolo*) of that village. He said that although he was a fisherman rather than a basket maker (some men also make baskets), he was an old man who had seen and learned many things in life; if I was interested, before leaving in March for the fishing camps on the Kashiji River, he would teach me the Luvale tradition.

Kakoma thus began describing in very lucid and gripping terms various details about basketry. Before long, knowing of my interest in basket divination, he smoothly shifted the conversation in that direction by connecting the weaving of baskets for the storage of food to the weaving of baskets for divining. He explained that a coiled basket used to store flour and a coiled basket used to divine are very different. The first one is narrow and deep; the second is wide and shallow. Although many women can make flour baskets, only those past childbearing age are allowed to weave divination baskets. Making and delivering an ordinary basket are straightforward processes, but that is not the case with a *lipele*.

Then, in a narrative style common among diviners, Kakoma began to explain how a man who lives an ordinary life one day becomes a diviner.

A divination basket is not created the day someone announces, "I'll receive an oracle and become a diviner." Oh no. First, a man falls sick and his relatives go to a diviner to consult his lipele. The diviner tells them that a deceased relative of theirs owned a lipele while he was alive, and that he now wishes to see it back in the village. The deceased relative is afflicting his descendant in the form of a spirit named Kay-ongo, because he wants him to fill the divination basket again.

So his maternal relatives go and give a deposit to the diviner who will fill and animate the new oracle. This diviner asks them, "Have you kept the oracle that belonged to your late relative?" If they respond that it was buried together with him, he goes on to tell them to commission a new one. To begin with, they should leave a piece of white clay

3. A flour basket coiled with *jikenge* roots (Museu Antropológico da Universidade de Coimbra, Portugal, cat. no. 79.65.19; photo by Carlos Barata)

[*pemba*] and a piece of red clay [*ngula*] at the doorway of a woman past childbearing age who knows how to make oracles [meaning the *lipele* coiled baskets, or *jimbango jalipele*]. They give her a deposit [*mwivwi*][2] and urge her to begin making the basket immediately. She replies that she feels too weary; they should go and dig up *jikenge*

roots themselves. [*Jikenge* are the roots from a semi-deciduous shrub or small tree called *mukenge* (*Combretum zeyheri*) (White 1961:6).]

So they go digging up *jikenge*. They take the roots to her village and she starts weaving their basket. She ties a knot with one root and begins to coil. The sides of this basket will be much shorter than those seen in other coiled baskets. The divination basket must be wide and flat to hold the *jipelo* and make them easy for the clients to see and the diviner to shake up during divination.

Once the basket maker has finished her work, she puts a piece of white clay and a piece of red clay inside the basket and sends out the message: "Take the dead person [*mufu*] you have given me." She calls the basket "dead person" because it is like the corpse [*chivimbi*] of the late diviner.[3]

The clients come to her village at dawn, before sunrise. The basket is lying in her doorway or in the kitchen hut. They just grab it and go, like thieves. She won't hand it over to them, no. Right where they find the oracle they leave a cloth, a blanket, or some money. Nowadays, they probably leave about ten thousand *kwachas*.[4] They please her with their generosity to ensure that she won't harm their oracle. And off they go.

When the basket maker wakes up, she starts looking for her basket. She curses [*kwangula*] the diviner who stole it, while striking the ground with a pole from the *mukenge* tree. This is how the oracle is received from the basket maker. She has to curse the diviner for the oracle to work.

A divination basket begins its biography as an ordinary coiled basket, made by a woman past childbearing age who masters the coiling technique. The basket maker makes the basket for a price and expects to be paid. This is an exchange in the subsistence sphere, and the Luvale speakers would probably concur that their *lipele*, much like the Kongo *minkisi* sculptures prior to ritual activation, is "anything but an object of utility, like a climbing loop or a mat" (MacGaffey 2000:82). Yet, few would deny that the *lipele* is an object of utility of a different order. Not only does it mediate, as commodities cannot, the creation of a social relationship between the basket maker and the diviner, but its weaving and delivery are accompanied by out-of-the-ordinary behavior. Hinting at this early transformation, diviner Sanjamba described the diviner who commissioned the basket as someone who is placed apart (*napu nge mutu wakujila*), someone who is prohibited from eating "bad fish" and other "bad things," and from being "sexually active." The basket maker herself is not allowed to engage in sexual intercourse for the duration of her work. Furthermore, the diviner cannot receive the basket directly from the basket maker; he must "steal the basket" (*kwiva mbango*) as if he were a thief, and the basket maker must "curse" him while she hits the ground with a *mukenge* pole.

Why must the diviner "steal" the basket and the basket maker "curse" the diviner? Cursing, according to Sanjamba, ensures that the *lipele* will "perform well and be powerful and fierce." The basket maker wishes death and misfortune to the diviner so that he and his *lipele* will be able to divine the causes of human suffering. Divination requires cursing. At the same time, cursing needs a material basis to be effective, hence the *mukenge* pole.[5] The choice of wood for making the pole is significant. The *mukenge*, a hardwood tree, stands for the implacable power of the curse, which is why it plays so central a role in *lipele* divination: the cursing pole, the divining basket, and the flattened spheres of the dumbbell-shaped divination rattle (*musambo*) are all made from *mukenge*.

Neither Sanjamba nor the other diviners had much to say about the ritual of stealing the basket, so I attempted to fill in the gap with an interpretation of my own. Could this ritual serve to mask what was essentially an economic transaction? Could it in effect engender the de-commoditization of the *lipele*?

The Weight of Silence

Following my meeting with fisherman Kakoma, I searched in vain for an elderly woman who made divination baskets. I had been told that only Mbunda and Luchazi women, few of whom live in Chavuma, weave baskets using *jikenge* roots. One morning, though, a messenger arrived with a missive from Sanjamba: "Meet me at the crossroads in Hakachi to go and meet a *lipele* maker." Surprised and bewildered, but very thankful all the same, I hurried to send back a note. I knew that in the highly secretive environment of Chavuma, where the names and identity of others are rarely revealed, I would have probably never met Pezo without Sanjamba.

Predictably, my meetings with Pezo were part of this environment of silence and suspicion. She and her husband, Ndonji, strived to hide their Angolan identity, quite correctly convinced that the less they said the fewer risks they ran. I knew from previous encounters with other Angolans that they would not welcome my curiosity about their past or the past of their objects. I had to phrase my thoughts and questions—including those pertaining to the activity that filled our meetings, basket making, which had at first appeared innocuous—with great caution. I never, for example, asked Pezo about where, when, and how she had learned her craft. This was not only because I knew that in all likelihood she had learned basket making while growing up in Angola by watching her mother or another female relative at work; rather, it was because my probing into the past would awaken disturbing memories of war and displacement.

I could not, however, ignore the cues betraying Pezo and Ndonji's nationality. I often identified Portuguese words in their speech, being a native speaker of Portuguese myself, and, on occasion, I heard conversations carried out in my presence about close relatives who had remained in Angola. Once an old man approached Ndonji to deliver fresh news from Ndonji's relatives in Lumege, Angola. On another occasion, Ndonji, Pezo, and an Angolan visitor introduced each other by mentioning their ethnic and clan affiliation, place of birth, and important stages of their biography as Angolan refugees. Ndonji described himself as a Luvale speaker of the Mbuze clan, born and raised near the Luena River. In 1966, following the death of his three classificatory brothers in a virulent clash between the MPLA and the Portuguese forces, he had trekked to Zambia through Cassupa and settled at his nephew's village in Lukolwe. After his two wives divorced him (many Angolan women divorced their Angolan husbands to marry Zambian men), he had married Pezo and moved to Hakachi. Pezo introduced herself as a Mbunda speaker of the Kamba clan, born near the Luio River. In 1966, she had followed her husband to Lutembo in Angola. In the late 1970s, caught in the crossfire between the MPLA and UNITA in independent Angola, they had run into the forest and hid there for two long years. In the 1980s, as the conflict intensified, they had been forced to cross the international border and settle near the Lungwebungu River. After her divorce, she moved to the village of close matrilineal relatives in Lukolwe, where she met Ndonji.

This is all I ever learned about Pezo and Ndonji's past. I wanted to ask them about the Luena River and the Luio River, how it had been to live in colonial Angola, and what it had taken to survive the war and walk the long way to Zambia. Their past experiences, however, were closed to me by the sheer force of fear.

Other kinds of silence proved difficult to unravel. Each time I asked Pezo a question on technique, I received the same polite but frugal answer: *Ngunakutunga mbango* (I'm coiling a basket). On rare occasions, she volunteered that she was weaving the basket's bottom or widening the walls, but she never offered detailed descriptions of her work or a summary of the weaving process from beginning to end. It was not easy to identify the reasons behind her silence, and I often imputed it, perhaps unfairly, to her husband's dominant personality. I had already encountered the same silence while working with other basket makers in Chavuma, however, so I began to wonder whether it could be explained not by Ndonji's personality or the politics of the district but by the nature of the activity itself. A skill like basket making is learned and taught by doing, not by talking. With this in mind, the technical descriptions to be offered shortly should be understood as resulting from my observations and modest basket-weaving experience, as well as from occasional conversations with basket makers other than Pezo.

Another kind of silence pertained to ritual. Pezo and Ndonji believed that I would form a better opinion of them if they omitted all traces of ritualization from *lipele* making, even though my research interest in divination suggested the reverse. Once Pezo claimed that the basket maker need not strike on the ground with a *mukenge* pole after the diviner "steals" her basket. As everyone else had told me differently, I said to myself that I would eventually discover the truth when a diviner came to "steal" his basket from Pezo. Would she curse him? Would she hit the ground with a *mukenge* pole? The delivery ceremony would solve the mystery. In the end, however, the mystery was never solved, and the only conclusion that I drew from the ceremony was a philosophical one: in ethnography, as everywhere, truth eludes us.

Pezo and Ndonji's insistence on purging ritualization from their behavior and descriptions had one more consequence. Of all possible ways for understanding the *lipele*, they chose the one that, in their view, made basket divination appear more secular. So they likened the *lipele* to a working tool, and they hid the equally important fact that the *lipele* is steeped in ritual and likened to a person.

When later, downplaying Pezo and Ndonji's interpretation, I came to interpret the ritual of stealing the basket as an act of de-commoditization, I felt uneasy because I knew that I was prioritizing Appadurai and Kopytoff's theory. Even if, as an anthropologist, one is not bound to the interpretations of those one studies, should not theory and fieldwork illuminate each other?

Ethnographic data that I collected later and which I describe and analyze in the following chapters, led me to revise my interpretation of the ritual of stealing the basket. Here, I describe the stages of conception and delivery in the biography of divination baskets as I came to understand them during my meetings with Pezo and Ndonji. In the process, I also share my coming to terms analytically with their interpretation of the *lipele* as a working tool.

Pezo Makes a Lipele for Sakutemba

12 September 1996

As Sanjamba had instructed me in writing, we met at the crossroads in Hakachi, Chavuma, to go and visit Pezo. We found Pezo lying on a mat next to her mud-brick house, chewing a twig and showing no intention of welcoming us. Ndonji offered us stools and guided us to the shade of a tree in the village yard. The young age of this tree and the minuscule size of his village and the houses in it—his and Pezo's, his son's, and his classificatory mother's—bespoke of Ndonji's recent arrival in Hakachi. Older villages exhibited mature, heavy-crowned trees, such as mango and avocado trees. These villages typically housed some ten to twenty individuals and were composed of a core of related men, their wives, their young children, some of their sisters' grown sons, and their divorced or widowed mothers and sisters. The villages of recent settlers were much smaller. When he arrived in Chavuma, having no matrilineal relatives to rely on, Ndonji had set up his village in the area of a fellow clansman. In the past, clan members had been known to provide shelter and protection to their visitors, but in the 1990s they did little more than grant the right to settle in their villages.[6] Many Angolan refugees had been forced to activate such undependable relationships. Some had even settled in the villages of their sisters' husbands or wives' relatives, submitting themselves to trying conditions of social impotency and marginality.

Cedric Chikunga, my second research assistant, introduced me briefly and explained my interest in divination baskets. Ndonji confirmed that his wife was a *lipele* maker, and he proceeded to list all the names of diviners whose baskets she had made, as if to validate her skill. A diviner who had returned to Angola in 1995 without ever having raised the money for the final payment had ordered her last basket. Ndonji asked Pezo to bring out this basket from the house. She forced her aged, frail body out of the shade and returned holding a soiled basket in one hand. She greeted us with a broad

4. Diviner Sakutemba (Chavuma, 2002; photo by author)

smile that showed the twig between her teeth. Now she seemed less impolite than nonchalant, and a little shy.

Soon after this visit with Pezo, a middle-aged diviner named Sakutemba called my attention to his *lipele*. He explained that he and his *lipele* had been divining the causes of human suffering for a long time and that now his basket had lost its shape, causing the *jipelo* to fall out with the upward shaking. Guessing his thoughts, or maybe projecting mine onto his, I proposed that he order a new one from Pezo. I myself would cover the expenses of transforming it into an oracle. Sakutemba gladly agreed. This arrangement pleased us both, and we sat down to discuss the details of what had to be done and purchased.

27 September 1996

I met Sakutemba and Cedric on the reddish gravel road. As we passed a quiet neighborhood, I gave Sakutemba a bill of five hundred *kwachas* for Pezo's deposit. We agreed that we should arrive separately at Ndonji's and behave as if we had never met. The problem, as Sakutemba saw it, was that otherwise Pezo would think that I was commissioning the basket, which would cause her to weave a smaller basket and skip the ritual steps. In response to my discomfort with deception, he asked if I would avoid sexual intercourse for an entire month if I knew that the final basket would never be consecrated. I saw his point. The efficacy of his future *lipele* was at stake.

I hurried ahead and reached Ndonji's in a short while. Ndonji offered me his tiny stool and guided me to the shade of his tree. As we prepared to sit down and exchange greetings, we saw Sakutemba approaching. Sakutemba greeted us politely by slightly clapping his hands while bending his knees. With the detachment of someone encountering strangers, he introduced himself to us as a diviner from Kalwiji, a residential area in Chavuma, and went on to inform Pezo and Ndonji that his *lipele* needed replacement. Pezo nodded and walked away. Ndonji responded that he had never heard of Sakutemba, but all the same he was very glad to learn that there was a diviner in Kalwiji. He would dig *jikenge* roots the next day and ensure that his wife worked hard on the basket.

Sakutemba reminded Ndonji that *lipele* initiations must take place before the rainy season, when farming takes priority. He would return the following week to check on Pezo's progress and to discuss such details as the final payment (*fweto*) and when and how to collect the basket. He gave the bill of five hundred *kwachas* to Ndonji, who put it in his shirt pocket. Then, as they shook hands in farewell, Sakutemba ventured a dash of humor: Would a fine basket maker such as Pezo remember when to finish the base and start weaving the sides? Would his *lipele* be the right size, or wide like a winnowing basket?

As Sakutemba walked down a narrow path that cut through an arid maize field, Ndonji shook his head in disapproval, clearly thinking that Sakutemba's shabby figure did not fit the portrait of a *lipele* diviner. There are two kinds of people in the world, Ndonji said: those who benefit from the gifts that God bestows on them and those who waste those gifts; those who always prosper, and those who always decline. Diviners are no exception. A *lipele* brings happiness and wealth to its owner. Diviners, however, are not necessarily wealthy. Some are men of wealth and importance (*vakaluheto*) whereas others will always be poor (*vakakuhutwa*). This, according to Ndonji, is because the wealthy use their gains wisely, buying cattle, marrying several women, and expanding their villages, whereas the poor fall for alcohol and lovers.

4 October 1996

Sakutemba arrived at Ndonji's in the late morning. He found me in the usual place, absorbed in Pezo's work. To begin the basket, Pezo had selected a thick *kenge* (singular of *jikenge*), which she had prepared with a knife by peeling off the root's brown skin and smoothing the exposed surface. This thick root, which becomes the core of a *kenge* basket, is called *mulinjiko*. Pezo grabbed an axe blade from the ground and tapered one end of the *mulinjiko* on a log. When the end became flexible, she tied it into a knot (*lihunda*). The Luvale proverb *Kaputu kambango kuvangila lihunda* (A coiled basket always begins

5. Bundles of *jikenge* roots, shaved and unshaved (Chavuma, 1996; photo by author)

with a knot), meaning that complications in life grow out of a small detail, refers to this initial knot. Basket makers refer to the tying of this knot as *kuputuka* (to begin).

Pezo began coiling the basket's bottom. She wound the thick core around the knot once, pierced the thick knot with an awl, and proceeded to lace a thin *kenge* thread through the hole in her direction. This *kenge* thread had been previously peeled, smoothed, split down the middle, and soaked in water for a few minutes to make it pliable. Next, she pierced another hole in front of the first and laced the thread through it; and so forth. When she reached the second turn of the spiral, she started interlocking this turn with the first. This circular movement of interlocking adjoining turns in a spiral is conveyed by the term *kujingulula* (to go around) or by the more general term *kutunga* (to make or build something with one's hands). Pezo tightened all her stitches evenly. Now and then, she splashed the work with water to keep the materials moist.

When the diameter of the basket's bottom had reached a width of about eight centimeters, Pezo began weaving the sides. This change of angle is conveyed by the term *kwimika* or *kwolola* (to straighten up). Always facing the inside of the basket and moving rightward, Pezo continued interlocking the two top rows with thin threads, which she kept moist and pliable by pulling them through her wet fingers.

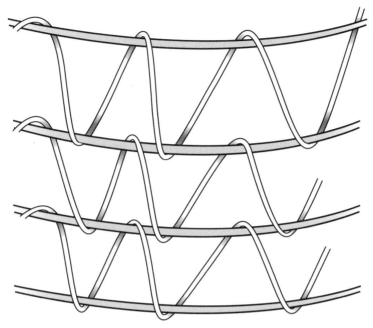

6. Single-foundation coiling (drawn by Sean D'Angelo)

Not realizing that Ndonji had described himself to me as a Zambian or maybe assuming that I would not understand the Luvale language, a passerby came to deliver fresh news from Ndonji's relatives in Lumege. Before Ndonji had the time to think how to keep up his Zambian persona, his visitor reported that he had found Ndonji's relatives in good health. Ndonji exuded surprise, happiness, and embarrassment all at once. We lapsed again into silence, each hoping that the other would pretend that nothing had been said and that I still believed that Ndonji was a Zambian. After some time, breaking the silence, Ndonji's classificatory mother complained of *lisolo* (a strong craving for meat and fish dishes) and wistfully reminisced about tasty caterpillars and *osamwina* (dried game meat). This initiated a lively conversation, as the Angolan refugees complained bitterly about the cassava-leaf dishes all too often eaten in Chavuma, a dietetic reminder of their dislocation and poverty.

At the mention of cassava leaves, Pezo rolled her eyes and eagerly ordered Sakutemba to "steal" his basket by the end of the month, probably hoping to use the money to buy tastier relishes. She reminded him that a close friendship (*usendo waunene chikuma*), comparable to the "*lipele* friendship"

7. Pezo coiling a *lipele* (Chavuma, 1996; photo by author)

that he already nursed with his fellow diviners, his wife, and his apprentice, would grow between them. Were she to find him shaking his *lipele* on her daily errands or occasional travels, she added with a contagious chuckle, she would approach him nonchalantly and take hold of his clients' divination payment. Sakutemba should also remember to pay her occasional visits and give her small gifts in recognition for her work. He should always remember the woman whose hands had made his working tool, for the divination spirit alone would not make him a diviner. Do spirits make baskets? she asked. As for the delivery of Sakutemba's basket, on a day to be scheduled, before sunrise, he should come to her village and steal it. He should leave a payment of ten thousand *kwachas* on her doorway. Cedric and Sakutemba seemed pleased with the price. They were not at all surprised with Pezo's juxtaposition of the language of stealing with the language of business.

Pezo's remarks gave me the longed-for opportunity to express my interest in attending the ceremony of stealing the basket and to mention the way fisherman Kakoma had described it to me. Ndonji listened attentively and then presented his own version:

> If a lipele is worn out, the diviner looks for an old woman who knows how to make lipele baskets. He pays her a visit and orders a basket. He gives her a deposit of five hundred kwachas. Soon thereafter, she goes into the bush to collect roots. When she finishes the basket, she sends a messenger to inform the diviner about the final price.
>
> On the arranged day, the diviner or one of his relatives goes to the basket maker's doorway to collect the basket. He grabs the basket and lays the final payment in the same spot. Then he leaves. Now, the basket maker starts cursing the diviner: "You who took my basket! Die with it! Go and die! Go to the red ground!" The exact words vary. At the same time, she hits the ground with a *mukenge* pole. That's all.

At this, Pezo intervened. Consistent with her denial of the role of ritualization in the weaving process, she said that she had never heard of anyone hitting the ground with a pole while cursing the diviner. She had reacted similarly on another occasion, when I had mentioned, quoting a local diviner, that the basket maker and her husband had to abstain from sexual intercourse for the duration of basket making. On this occasion, however, Ndonji and others who had joined the group contradicted her. One man asked her in response: "Would not a woman whose crops were stolen from her field curse the thief while striking the ground with a *mukenge* pole?"

16 October 1996

I noticed that Pezo had continued weaving the basket walls during our absence. She had created a thick ridge about three centimeters from the bottom by weaving over her last row at a sharp diagonal. This ridge, *mukungu*, which resembles and is named after the top of some thatched roofs, is said to strengthen the basket and prevent the divining articles from flying out with the upward shaking. Pezo had also continued weaving above the first ridge, following the same method as she had used below it. At the sixth turn above the ridge and for the next five or six rows, she had laced the weaver around three rows at regular intervals, creating successive sets of two graceful parallel lines diagonal to the rim. This decorative motif is called *mishi* (pounding poles). I asked Pezo if she knew the names of any other designs used in divination baskets or other baskets coiled with *jikenge* roots, but she remained silent.

Today, having completed the pounding-poles design and steadily widened the basket sides, Pezo added a second thick ridge. When, hours later, the basket resembled a tureen about eight centimeters deep and thirty centimeters wide, she wove another row in the usual way, and then proceeded to fill the gaps between the stitches of this top row by wrapping it with a *kenge* thread for the second time but now without interlocking this row with the

8. A new *lipele* woven by Pezo (Chavuma, 1996; photo by author)

previous one. This careful weaving and embellishing of the last row, common in all kinds of coiled baskets, is known in Luvale as *kukukula*. The term conveys the idea of finishing, trimming, or clipping, as one does to the branches of a tree (Horton 1953:136).

Ndonji passed a pipe with tobacco to Pezo. She had a big puff and then announced the completion of her work: *Yinakumu lyehi* (Finished). Ndonji remarked that the basket would have taken much longer to make had Sakutemba been less worried with the approaching rains, the same being true for any baskets coiled early in the rainy season, when farming takes priority. Ndonji was clearly pleased with the quality of Pezo's work.

Then Ndonji held the basket with both hands and shook it as diviners do. It feels right, he said. Spinning the basket on his knee, he directed my attention to its shape as he delivered a few words of wisdom: "See how similar it is to other coiled baskets? They are all *vikwachilo* [containers]." Pezo also insisted that all coiled *kenge* baskets are the same, and she went on to remind me that as a basket maker who uses *jikenge* roots to coil both divination baskets and food baskets she knew it well.

My first reaction to this statement was to explain it away with the couple's recurring need to portray the *lipele* as an ordinary basket. It seemed clear to me that the differences between divination baskets and food baskets were much more striking than the similarities, being amply supported by sound, even visible, ethnographic facts. For example, although some food baskets are also made of *jikenge* roots, they are much taller than divination baskets and have no ridges. Other food baskets are made of grass, palm skeins, or bark rope, and their decorative motifs are so diverse and colorful that the *kenge* baskets look dull in comparison. Over time, a coiled food basket sold to a woman is likely to exhibit a thin layer of foodstuff, often white flour, whereas a *lipele* sold to a diviner is rubbed with empowering substances and slightly bent inward. The two kinds of baskets are also treated very differently once they have outlived their usefulness: An old food basket is simply discarded and left around the neighborhood to decay. A divination basket, on the contrary, ought to be buried beside the river or on top of an anthill.[7] A flour basket is harmless; a *lipele* is very dangerous, especially to women and children.

I proceeded to conceptualize these differences in terms of the dichotomy between commodities and personified objects: a woman's basket is a commodity that is exchangeable for something else, whereas a diviner's *lipele*, being a thing endowed with human-like qualities such as volition and thought, is excluded from economic exchange. The ethnography corroborated the interpretation, and the interpretation illuminated the ethnography. It all made good sense.

I could not, however, ignore the stress on similarity. How could I explain the common tendency to regard the differences, which were also recognized at the technical and functional levels, as less important than the similarities? How could I conceptualize this? Unwilling at this point of my intellectual trajectory to part from commoditization theory, I suddenly realized that I could interpret the stress on similarity with the same theory that I had used to conceptualize my stress on difference. I reminded myself that in Appadurai's and Kopytoff's views, commoditization and personification are inverse images of the same phenomenon, singularities being commodities *in potentia* (the case of divination baskets) and commodities ending up on occasion in ritual enclaves (the case of winnowing baskets, for example, which may be reused for ritual purposes during the boys' initiation ceremony, never again reverting to their original function). I surmised that it is this potential that makes divination baskets and food baskets similar. In a way, as Appadurai notes, they are both commodities.

Stealing the Basket

17 OCTOBER 1996

I met Sakutemba around 5:30 A.M. to go and steal his basket from Pezo. Sakutemba wore a brown blazer for the occasion and woolen pants with torn knees. To excuse my tardiness, I explained that a mile down the road, realizing that my dog was following me, I had been forced to cycle back home. Cedric reported that Sakutemba had already stolen the basket, fearing that the sun would rise before my arrival. This news came as a jolt. I could not believe that I had missed the delivery ceremony, and all because of my dog. Could we repeat it? I asked hesitantly. The idea seemed absurd, but I could not think of a better alternative. To my relief, Sakutemba kindly consented. He told Cedric to run ahead and inform Pezo. The two of us followed.

We found Cedric seated on a blue sofa chair in the middle of the deserted village, a surreal sight. Ndonji had worried that I might arrive too early and need a rest. I would have been happy with his small stool, but maybe a sofa befitted the occasion. Sakutemba walked toward Pezo's doorway. He put the basket back on her doorstep and, for the second time that day, he collected it and hid it in a plastic bag. He laid the two bills of five thousand *kwachas* that I had earlier slipped into his blazer pocket on the same spot and weighted them down with a stone. Then he walked away toward the road.

9. Bear, my dog (Chavuma, 1996; photo by author)

Soon after Sakutemba disappeared beyond the parched maize field, Ndonji opened the door and collected the money. He was immediately followed by Pezo, clad in a colorful *chitenge* cloth round her waist, a bright yellow jacket, and a red scarf about the head. Hunched against the chill of dawn, she walked across the village, cursing Sakutemba all the while. She halted twenty feet down the narrow sand path leading to the main road and continued cursing. She did not hit the ground with a *mukenge* pole or any other pole. Then she turned around and burst into laughter. "Have you brought those scones and tea you promised?" she asked. "It's so cold this morning."

One month later, I described this ceremony to a respected Chokwe diviner named Sangombe. Sitting on a woven chair in the front room of my thatched-roof house, Sangombe reacted to my account as follows:

Sangombe: The basket maker cuts a small *mukenge* pole in the bush. You approach her house while she is still asleep. After you leave, she walks toward your footprints. She's treating [*kuka*] the oracle. A *lipele* oracle is not received in silence, oh no. She confirms that you're out of sight, pauses for a brief instant, and starts looking for her basket. "Where's my basket?" A fellow villager replies, "You've already sold it!" So she grabs the pole and starts insulting the diviner. She stands by his footprints and hits the pole on the ground. Thud! "Hope your wife dies!" Thud! "Your child dies!" Thud! "Your mother dies!" Thud! She hits the *mukenge* pole on the ground near his footprints, facing east. She feels tired.

Me: What happens to the oracle if she doesn't curse the diviner?

Sangombe: She cursed him; she cursed him. The diviner doesn't collect the basket and walk away in silence, no! A diviner goes back home and fills his oracle. But he may return to the basket maker's village to ask: "Have you cursed this *lipele*?" "No, I haven't," she confesses. "So, curse it now!" he orders. Yes, she cursed Sakutemba. Thud! Thud! "Hope you die! Hope your wife breaks her head! Hope your child dies!" And so on. A *lipele* that is not cursed by the basket maker cannot divine. It must be cursed first. Yes, a *lipele* only brings difficulties.

Me: Pezo cursed Sakutemba's *lipele*, but she didn't hit the ground with the pole.

Sangombe: What?!

Cedric: She cursed him as she walked down the path. "You've stolen my basket! Hope you die! Hope you disappear!" And so on, all those insults . . .

Sangombe: She did curse his oracle! After you left, she carried her pole and started cursing. She waited for your departure. Ask her and she will say, "Yes, I cursed him with the pole." The basket maker is a fellow villager. She will become known as the one who made so-and-so's *lipele*. A diviner cannot do without a *lipele*. My son inherited my *lipele*. He is eating your money. Every day his heap of money grows higher. His clients cover him with riches. A *lipele* is coiled before being filled. And if you want me to fill it, pay me first. Money is satanic [*mali atwama nasatana*].

Sangombe's insistence that Pezo struck the ground with a *mukenge* pole while cursing Sakutemba reminded me of another meeting in which we had discussed the way consulters introduce themselves to diviners. He had told me that consulters approach diviners by saying *Tuneza nakukuvila mungwa* (We've come to receive solid salt [into our mouths]) or *Tuneza nakulya mungwa* (We have come to eat salt). In this way, the consulters informed the diviners that they were on good terms, came for divining, and recognized the diviners' power as givers of salt—much like the peoples of the Upper

Zambezi, an area without salt-pans, had done during the Atlantic trade when they approached the Ovimbundu traders who carried sea salt in their loads— hence, the Luvale proverb *Kwambulula chimbali namungwa wenyi* (Before talking, do as the Ovimbundu trader with his salt).[8] When Cedric and I commented that in the 1990s consulters were more likely to say, rather blatantly, that they came for divining, Sangombe shook his head in disapproval; people knew what diviners expected from them.

I continued fueling conversations about the *mukenge* conundrum for a short while, until I began to wonder whether the distinction between what had happened and what should have happened really mattered. The more questions I asked, the more unclear the truth became. Pezo stated that she had not hit the ground with a *mukenge* pole while cursing Sakutemba. Sangombe and everyone else said she did. Would she risk crippling Sakutemba's *lipele*? Perhaps she had performed the rite when Sakutemba stole the basket the first time. Had my dog not delayed me, I would have known that. Or perhaps she waited for my departure to curse Sakutemba, as Sangombe reasoned.

A Way of Working and Laboring

Through the fog of silence and the difficulties of fieldwork, a fundamental if obvious fact emerged: the oracle is a basket. This realization is not simply a matter of ethnographic perfectionism or a compensation for the tendency to focus on the basket's contents and their symbolism in detriment of the basket;[9] this realization is at the very core of basket divination as a way of working and laboring.

In what follows, departing from commoditization theory, I reconcile myself with my fieldwork experience and explore the analytical consequences of taking very seriously what Pezo and Ndonji told me. I start with the names that the Luvale speakers have for coiled baskets, which they apply interchangeably, then I link the embodicd experience of weaving baskets to the social perception of these baskets as tools or organs that extend the human body into the material world. I close this chapter by placing the perception of basket divination as work and labor in the historically contingent reality of forced displacement.

Baskets and the Body

As mentioned earlier, the general term in the Luvale language for a coiled basket is *mbango*. The coiled baskets that women use for the storage and transportation of food can be more fully described as *jimbango jamapwevo* (women's coiled baskets). Divination baskets are most strictly defined as *jimbango jalipele* (*lipele* coiled baskets), until they have been personified in the course of a ritual ceremony that transforms them into *jingombo jalipele* (*lipele* oracles). Sangombe and fisherman Kakoma, however, loosely described the divination basket prior to its consecration as *ngombo* (oracle). The converse is at least as frequent, people referring to the *lipele* oracle simply as a basket. People use these terms loosely and interchangeably without need for qualification or hedging ("loosely speaking" or "strictly speaking," for example) even though they acknowledge that a basket differs from an oracle. Not only do people know that the context of conversation will clarify any possible semantic ambiguity or misunderstanding, but they seem to act on the assumption that the *lipele* is ontologically ambiguous at every stage of its biography: in the same way that the sacredness of the *lipele* is expressed in the rites that accompany the basket weaving and delivery, its materiality as a woven basket permeates its adulthood. In the first case, the basket is already an oracle; in the second, the oracle is still a basket.

This helps begin to explain why, in Pezo and Ndonji's opinion and experience, divination baskets can be described as *jimbango* regardless of their different teleological functions—divining or assisting in the preparation of food. But there is more to it than the loose application of names that reflect ontological ambiguity. The human body—here the basket maker's and the basket user's—is also a locus of experience (Jackson 1989; Stoller 1989b, 1997). For the artisan, all coiled *kenge* baskets, including the *lipele*, require the same habitual postures, movements, and sensory recognitions. When coiling a basket, women sit on a flat surface, often a woven mat, their legs outstretched and their backs vertical. They use their teeth to help tie the starting knot; they recognize the smell and texture of moist materials; they know how to guide the spiraling core, how strongly to push the awl, how tightly to pull the threads, and how to shape the basket walls. They know all this because their bodies have learned it through mimesis and repetition.

Furthermore, the making of all coiled baskets is conceived directly as growth. The basket maker begins the basket (*kuputuka*) with a knot; she straightens up the walls (*kwimika*) and makes the basket grow (*kutohwesa* or *kusokesa*) and widen (*kwala*); and, finally, she weaves the last row (*kukukula*). The more she takes her threads around the spiral, the more the basket grows. This slow process of growth evokes other fields of mundane activity equally grounded in primary bodily experiences: the basket maker "begins" a basket like a man "begins" a mud-brick house. She "straightens up" the basket like she helps someone "stand up." She "enlarges" the basket like she "fattens" (*kutohwesa*) a child or like a plant "sprouts" (*kusoka*). She "finishes" the basket like one "trims" branches from a tree. The art of basket making is perceived and experienced as one expression of the vast, bodily process of making things (*kutunga*). The basket maker is a maker of things, a *mukakutunga*. In fact, in the Luvale and related languages there are no special words for *basketry, basket making, basket maker*, or even *basket*.

In addition to calling for the same raw materials, the same skills, the same postures, the same sensory recognitions, and the same experiential resonance with other manual activities, divination baskets and food baskets are similarly perceived as tools that fit and extend the human body. Even if divination and the preparation of food are very different activities, coiled baskets, as Ndonji said, are all containers (*vikwachilo*). They are instruments that are equally adapted to the human anatomy, their concave bodies holding fragments of the world. The basket users cannot feel whether those fragments are smooth, jagged, or sticky, but they are able to feel their weight and mass through the baskets—Don Ihde's "terminus" of one's "intentional extension into the world" (1979:7).[10] In this process, the basket withdraws from perception; it becomes an extension of the hands. Drew Leder writes that "natural organs are modified and supplemented via the incorporation of such artificial extensions" (1990:33). Karl Marx had earlier described working tools as "prolongations" of the human body, and the ancient Greeks had earlier still encapsulated this symbiotic relationship in one single world, *organon*, meaning both the bodily organ and the tool (Marx 1964:89).

In passing, this also helps explain why people in Chavuma sometimes refer to a *lipele* as a winnowing basket, or *lwalo*. At first, once again, I found the differences between these two types of baskets to be more striking than the similarities: women coil a *lipele* with *jikenge* roots, whereas men plait a *lwalo* with reed splints, bark-rope, and wooden rods; men use *lipele* baskets for divining, whereas women use *lwalo* baskets for winnowing. Yet a *lipele* is a *lwalo* because both baskets share two quintessential physical traits—openness and shallowness—which enable them to share as well similar motor-activity properties. Divination baskets and winnowing baskets are both intended to be held with both hands and shaken. Their "inherent properties" matter less than their "interactional properties," which are defined by the way the human body interacts with them (Lakoff and Johnson 1980:122-23). Even if winnowing grains with a *lwalo* (*kupepa*) and shaking a *lipele* (*kusekula*) are very different activities, these baskets extend the human body into the world in a similar way. For the human body, a *lipele* really is a *lwalo*.

10. Rose Chikunga winnowing rice with a *lwalo* (Chavuma, 2002; photo by author)

The importance of bodily and sensory experiences does not end here, however. I quickly realized that the privileging of similarity over difference also stemmed from what people in Chavuma experienced as an inescapable imperative of life—the satisfaction of bodily needs.

This idea was first brought home to me as I administered a questionnaire. One question asked what a *lipele* is used for. Everyone replied that a *lipele* is used for divining. Another question asked whether the *lipele* had any "special meaning" or was endowed with any "special qualities" that differentiated it from other ordinary objects. Everyone replied that a *lipele* has no special qualities. One day, I decided to explain to an interviewee why one question differed from the other, a challenging exercise, it turned out. He listened attentively, then retorted that the Luvale have a handful of important objects: axes and hoes, mortars and pestles, cooking pots and cooking sticks, and baskets and mats. The Luvale, he said, use axes and hoes for cultivating, mats for drying cassava in the sun, mortars and pestles for pounding dried cassava, baskets for storing it, and cooking pots and sticks for preparing cassava *shima* (regional staple food similar in consistency to stiff mashed potatoes). I pointed out that he had excluded the *lipele* from his list, which

11. An Angolan diviner shaking his *lipele* (Museu Nacional de Etnologia, Portugal; photo by Benjamin Pereira in Dundo, Angola, 1971)

to me seemed highly significant. He insisted that those objects are all equally useful—all things to work with and live off—the only difference being that a *lipele* is used for divining. For this man, clearly, the concept of usefulness is inseparable from the concept of subsistence, the toil and trouble of sustaining life. A *lipele* is similar to pots, axes, and mats, because, in his words, these are all *vyakuyoyesa* (fabricated things that make living possible). Pezo once conveyed the same idea as she compared divination baskets with food baskets: *vyakuzachisa vyakukafwa mujimba* (they are both useful things that assist the human body), she said.

Work and Labor

In the Luvale language, an important distinction is drawn between *kuzata* (to work), a derivation of which is *kuzachisa* (to use), and *milimo* (labor), a noun derived from the verb *kulima*, today used in the sense of cultivating. Divining is "work" because the *lipele*, a useful instrument, produces divinatory knowledge in the form of *jipelo* configurations. Inasmuch as abstract knowledge becomes materialized in configurations that result from the act of shaking a basket, the diviner must use his skilled hands like any other worker. Divining is manual work, and the product of this work represents a contribution to the artificial world of things, the "human artifice," even if only for the fleeting interval between consecutive shakes of the basket. Hannah Arendt's thoughts on works of art are worth quoting here:

> Works of art are thought things, but this does not prevent their being things. The thought process by itself no more produces and fabricates tangible things, such as books, paintings, sculptures, or compositions, than usage by itself produces and fabricates houses and furniture. The reification which occurs in writing something down, painting an image, modeling a figure, or composing a melody is of course related to the thought which preceded it, but what actually makes the thought a reality and fabricates things of thought is the same workmanship which, through the primordial instrument of human hands, builds the other durable things of the human artifice. (1958:169)

The same holds true for basket divination. As with the writer's pen, the dentist's probe, and the basket maker's awl, the *lipele* is the diviner's tool, and divining is manual work.

In addition to being work, though, divining is also labor in the sense that it caters to the needs of the human body. Like the English word "labor," the Luvale word *milimo* evokes the idea of tilling, cultivating, and travailing against the grain.[11] To labor as a diviner is to struggle to survive, attending daily to the satisfaction of bodily needs.

Here is how Sangombe described his "daily work":

> My daily work is to live the life of a diviner, attending to my needs as an embodied person [*kuzata chamulikumbi chakutwama nakuyoya changombo nakuyoya chamujimba wamutu*]. I live as I am living right now, and thus I have done for a long time. Those who remember me

will say, "Let's go to Sangombe's *lipele*." They come, you shake the basket for them, and they give you money. Sometimes, out of compassion, you give them back some money for paying their visit to a doctor. I do not eat all my patients' money, uh-uh. If there are no clients, you just stay in the village, one day after the other. The clients may come today, tomorrow, or after tomorrow; but they will come. This is the way.

The same theme appears in Sangombe's description of the ritual procedure for burying individuals linked to the *lipele*. Following the death of an apprentice who never shook a *lipele*, his master rubs red clay on his nose, tucks a powerless *kaponya* (wooden divinatory article) in his hand, and then says, "I gave you your name [meaning the *pumba* title given to apprentices], and now you have departed. This is your wooden article. Go *pumba*, take your *lipele* with you. My *lipele* remains behind, for me to make a living [*kuyoyamo*]." The same occurs at the death of Nyaminenge, the title given to the diviner's wife (or senior wife in the case of a polygynic family). Having rubbed red clay on her nose and tucked a wooden article in her hand, the diviner addresses his dead wife: "I've divided this *lipele* between us, so you can take your share. I remain here with my share, earning some shillings [meaning *kwachas*], raising my children."

It is worth mentioning that the distinction made in the Luvale language between the etymologically unrelated but experientially close terms *kuzata* (to work) and the noun *milimo* (labor), which derives, as mentioned, from the verb *kulima* (to cultivate), is also evident in several European languages: *ergazesthai* and *ponein* in ancient Greek, *facere* or *fabricari* and *laborare* in Latin, *travailler* and *oeuvrer* in French, and *werken* and *arbeiten* in German (Arendt 1958:80). To a contemporary English speaker, however, "work" has come to be associated with the world of wages and alienation from the products of one's labor, in sharp opposition to leisure (Applebaum 1992), and "labor" with unskilled occupations. In this light, a diviner would hardly qualify as a worker and a laborer. He would fit better the profile of a priest, a ritual expert, a diviner, a man with a vocation.

So it is that Western scholars, highly skilled professionals by vocation, at least in principle, have portrayed African diviners in their own image—as ritual experts, masters of ceremony, artists, and even scientists. This has led to ignoring the profits that diviners so commonly fetch as extraneous and dull. And, although this omission is a refreshing alternative to the old, scornful portrait of diviners as masters of sleight-of-hand who deceive their clients and live off them, it is hardly advisable.

In mid-1990s Chavuma, basket divination was perceived as ritual and work at one and the same time. This meant not only that the ritual and the practical were tightly interwoven, as Bronislaw Malinowski shows for the highly ritualistic yam gardening and canoe building in the Trobriand Islands (1948:8-18; see also Tambiah 1990:70-71), but also, and more important, that the Angolan diviners saw their work as they did plowing a field or making a basket. For them, divination was work and labor, a means of providing for themselves and their kin.

This overt materialism brings to mind Marx and Engels's thoughts on the production of the means of subsistence; they say, "Life involves before every-thing else eating and drinking, housing, clothing and various other things. The first historical act is thus the production of the means to satisfy these needs, the production of material life itself. And indeed this is a historical act, a fundamental condition of all history, which today, as thousands of years ago, must daily and hourly be fulfilled merely in order to sustain human life. Even when the sensuous world is reduced to a minimum, to a stick as with Saint Bruno, it presupposes the action of producing this stick" (1976:43-44). For the diviners, as for Marx, there were good reasons not to reify the distinc-tion between skilled and unskilled occupations, and intellectual and manual ones. For them, work and labor were dialectically and symbiotically related, being a function of life itself.

In Historical Perspective

The understanding of ritual as work and labor is not unique to northwest Zambia. In many societies, from the Ancient Hindu and pre-Christian Greeks to the present Bamana, Songhay, and Ndembu, ritual is described as "work." The very word *liturgy* is derived from the Greek *leos* or *laos* (the people) and *ergon* (work) (Turner 1982:30-31). Neither is the understanding of basket divination as work and labor historically recent. In 1875, during his travels through the Angolan province of Bié, Verney Cameron came upon a *lipele* consultation. He reports that first there was a "monotonous recitative" (the invocation stage of the divinatory speech) and, "this being finished, the soothsayer was ready to be consulted, provided those coming to him were prepared to pay in advance for his predictions" (1877:403). It is no coinci-dence that the word used for the divinatory payment, *chikoli*, derives from the verb *kukola*, to become strong. In the 1930s, Leona Tucker recorded an Ovimbundu song in Angola in which a basket diviner links divination to bodily contentment (1940:178):

I didn't say, "Come and get me,"
You yourself were ill.
Oh, my fellow diviners,
Hunger hurts.

In 1990s Chavuma, however, the understanding of basket divination as work and labor gained a new historical and existential significance. In the 1940s, diviners were in the habit of calling themselves "doctors" (*chimbuki*, *nganga*, or *chimbanda*). "The modern diviner," Charles White reported in 1947, "likes to stress the medical side of his profession and insist that he is purely a doctor and that whatever he does is to heal the sick" (1947:12). Diviners were desperately attempting to legitimize their work in the eyes of the British, who meanwhile had severely curtailed the practice of basket divination by introducing legislation against witchcraft and witch hunting. Many diviners moved to Angola, practiced in secret, or turned to more innocuous oracles, such as mirrors and pounding poles (Turner 1975/1961:243, White 1948c:95). In the 1990s, however, the situation in northwest Zambia had changed. Although the reformed Witchcraft Act continued to prohibit witchcraft accusations, diviners were now witnessing the renaissance of their profession and its official recognition by the Traditional Healers and Practitioners Association. It is ironic that the same oracles that had been previously banned were now enabling the diviners to rebuild their lives as refugees. The Angolan diviners put their skill to good use. Their baskets helped them regain social prestige, political influence, and economic advantage; in that process, their baskets helped them regain as well a degree of sociality, agency, and well-being—a fuller sense of personhood. These diviners were no longer describing themselves as doctors; now, they were workers and laborers.

How exactly the tool remade the worker I cannot tell. The majority of diviners crossed the border in the late 1960s, decades before I began my fieldwork, and they showed no interest in describing those years to me because doing so would be to disclose their refugee status. The work of other anthropologists who conducted fieldwork in Chavuma in the early 1970s, however, is revealing. Anita Spring reports that among the Angolan newcomers were traditional midwives, doctors, and diviners who were "interested in performing the rituals properly . . . to gain income as practitioners" (1982:43). Art Hansen contrasts those refugees who acquired food by doing agricultural labor in the fields of others with those who engaged in more lucrative activities, such as trading, crafts, and ritual professions. In Hansen's words,

"Engaging in more lucrative activities permitted the refugee to more rapidly accumulate wealth and to devote more time to other noneconomic activities that paid off in personal prestige, validation of status, and higher rank" (1982:29). Although most Angolan refugees had no other choice than to live hand-to-mouth for several years, specialized knowledge enabled a few to prosper. In the case of basket diviners, social recognition was nicely complemented with high earnings.

Yet, despite undeniable success, diviners continued to bemoan their plight in the 1990s. Day after day, they struggled to remake what the war stole from them, and they looked forward to the moments of happiness when, after a laborious session of work, they could enjoy the taste of abundance. Their self-portrayal as workers and laborers reflected this sense of constant struggle. Unlike researchers, who often live in niches of comfort and abundance, the diviners could not indulge in the luxury, because a luxury it is, of pretending that their profession stood above the imperatives of survival.

The Thing Stolen

Here we must return to the ritual of stealing the basket. I remind you that the basket maker charges the diviner for her work, and the diviner pays her, even though he is expected to "steal" the basket on a day to be scheduled. I mentioned earlier that no one had much to say about the meaning of this ritual besides referring me to the Luvale tradition—their ancestors who can no longer talk—and that I rushed to fill the void with an interpretation of my own: The diviner may have paid for the basket, but the *lipele* is no mere commodity. By sequestering the basket, the diviner removes it from the path of commoditization and symbolically redefines its value.

As conceptually sound and thought provoking as this interpretation is, however, I soon realized that it misses the ethnographic specificity of basket divination. From the perspective of long-range commoditization theory, the *lipele* begins its life as a commodity, moves on to spend its adulthood in ritual enclaves as an ex-commodity, and may one day return to the commoditization path as a museum or collector's specimen. From the perspective of the diviners and their clients, however, the *lipele* is not a commodity, an ex-commodity, or a potential commodity; the *lipele* it is a working tool. It is because the *lipele* is a working tool and a means of production that it is worth stealing.

Appadurai urges us to move away from the Marxian concern with production and embrace Georg Simmel's view of exchange as the source of economic value (1986a). My fieldwork, however, compelled me to reconsider the insights that production may offer. The cultural consumption of divination baskets—their use as oracles—is understood as an act of production. Given that this act of production requires the use of the hands to shake a basket, divining is manual work, comparable to winnowing grain, cultivating the land, or hunting game. The sacred baskets are tools, and the ritual of divination is work and labor.

In summary, as simple an assertion as "*the* lipele *is woven*" is pregnant with insights. The *lipele* is as much about animating and making sacred a material object as about involving it in the profane world. For the diviners and their clients, an account that portrays *lipele* divination exclusively as an intellectual exercise, an arrangement of symbols, or a ritual performance would seem bizarre to say the least. Being a ritualist is commensurate with being a worker and a laborer. The world of materiality and the somatic belong in the study of ritual, and our writings should be attuned to the practices, experiences, ideas, concerns, and biographies of those whom they describe. Although local forms of pragmatism should not deter us from approaching divination from the perspective of rationality, symbolism, and ritual action, they do urge us to not lose sight of life as lived. The understanding of *lipele* divination as work and labor does not make it less rational, symbolic, and ritual; rather, it impels us to take local experiences seriously and to show with vivacity how reason, symbols, and ritual are an integral part of the everyday.

2

Initiation

On the same day Sakutemba stole the basket from basket maker Pezo, he had it initiated into a mature oracle during a nightlong ritual. Basket divination led me from one ritual to another ritual. In addition to being a way of making a living, basket divination was also a way of doing things through ritual. The more I traced the biography of divination baskets, following them as they moved in space, the deeper I entered into liminal arenas and the clearer it became that the significance of the *lipele* could not be captured by such terms as *ex-commodity* and *enclaved commodity*.

It is, therefore, hardly surprising that it was here, in the realm of ritual, where I came to a fuller understanding of the act of stealing that had so intrigued me. Why do the diviner and the basket maker enact the delivery of the newborn *lipele* as an act of stealing? Why does the basket maker accuse the diviner of stealing her basket, calling him a thief? I mentioned in Chapter 1 that the diviners had nothing to tell me about the meaning of this ritual beyond referring to the weight of tradition. Other divination rituals, however, spoke volumes. The act of stealing, it turned out, was part of a larger contested history of male political encroachment into female domains, an encroachment symbolized by the stealing of a powerful and productive object.

From Women to Men

According to the Luvale chiefly epic, the first act of stealing and political encroachment took place long ago in Musumba, the Northern Lunda capital in the southwest corner of present-day Democratic Republic of the Congo. While the legendary chiefess Luweji was secluded in the menstruation hut, her husband, a Luba hunter by the name of Ilunga, seized her royal insignia, making himself the new chief of Musumba. Humiliated and enraged, her brothers Chinyama and Chinguli decided to leave. Chinguli headed west to found the Mbangala people; Chinyama and his followers traveled south, leading over the centuries to the formation of such peoples as the Luvale, Chokwe, and Luchazi. (The chiefly epics of these peoples describe in great detail how these processes unfolded over time.)[1] Meanwhile, back in Musumba, Ilunga consolidated his power. As Luweji would not conceive, he married a second wife named Kamongalwaza who bore him a daughter and two sons. One of these sons, Yavwa Nyaweji, became the first Northern Lunda king, Mwachiyavwa.

This said, it is important to realize that most Luvale in Chavuma know very little about the epic of Chinyama, their paramount chief, a fact probably related to the low degree of centralization of their precolonial politics.[2] Similarly, the average person in Chavuma and even the diviners show very little interest in the origins and diffusion of the *lipele*. Surprised as I was with the diviners' lack of curiosity, I soon realized that they found my surprise equally bewildering, even though they had come to accept my insatiable curiosity about their culture—a curiosity they saw as typical of non-Africans of the type "researcher." (The remaining non-African types, usually uninterested in their ways, were the missionary, the development worker, and the diamond smuggler.) One day, a century-old Angolan diviner named Samafunda, who had run to Zambia in the early twentieth century to escape forced labor, asked me, "Where has the hoe come from? Do you know where the axe and the knife have come from? Do you know the man who built the first house?" All these things had happened before him, and no one had told him about them.

The diviners, however, do know about the origins of *lipele* divination. I was told that the first oracle on earth was a wooden pestle (*mwishi*), which the primordial couple Nyamutu and Samutu gave to a woman named Nyakweleka.[3] This woman—a Luvale or Lunda, the opinions diverged—divined with her pestle on top of an anthill in the Inkalanyi valley, near Musumba, an area often referred to metonymically as Mwachiyavwa. One day Nyakweleka wove a basket from *kenge* roots as "requested" by her husband, never again divining with her oracle. Sakweleka, a Luvale, became the first *lipele* diviner.

Here is how diviner Sangombe described Nyakweleka:

Nyakweleka lived in Mwachiyavwa. She was neither Luchazi nor Luvale nor Mbunda nor Kangala nor Yayuma nor Chokwe nor Lwimbi nor Koya nor Chawa, uh-uh; she was a Lunda from Mwachiyavwa. The first oracle originated in Lundaland. As we say during the invocation (*kukombela*), "Quick quick quick, Nyakweleka divined with a pestle on top of an anthill. She came from Mwachiyavwa, Lundaland." The first oracle belonged to a woman, not to a man. They quarreled over it.

Nyakweleka started her divination sessions by invoking herself, "Quick quick quick, Nyakweleka is the woman who divines with a pestle; she is from Mwachiyavwa, Lundaland." Her clients would say, "Nyakweleka, divine our affliction [*chisako*]." She would ask her pestle, "What have they come for? Explain, oracle. Have they come for their animals or for something else? In their village there is a dog, a chicken, a duck, and a canary in a cage. What do these things mean?" She would pull the pestle, twi! . . . If, say, a youth stole food from a pot, he would stare at her pestle in fear, waiting for the moment it would take off in his direction. The youth would try to escape, but the pestle would go on hitting him. Twi! It would tear his skin, open his belly, and lift him up in the air. Pa! This oracle had no mercy. It belonged to Nyakweleka.

One day her husband, Sakweleka, said to her, "Woman, you must make a coiled basket!" She coiled the basket and then said to him, "The bow belonged to a woman and was taken from her by a man. I Nyakweleka am a woman. I've divined with a pestle on top of an anthill in the land of Mwachiyavwa, Nyakapamba Musopa, and Chinyama chaMukwamayi Kasongo waKumanyima [the praise name (*lijina lyamituto*) of the first Luvale chief, Chinyama]."[4] Nyakweleka coiled the basket. She spread out its sides, as her husband had instructed her. (Her basket resembled the one that Pezo wove for diviner Sakutemba.) Sakweleka filled the basket with some charcoal and various bits of wood. He shook it. He threw in a manioc tuber. He shook it again, and the tuber came on top.

One day Sakweleka collapsed. Nyakweleka asked her pestle to name the ancestral spirit who had seized her husband. The pestle became stock-still, so she said, "It's Kayongo! It's Kayongo! Bring the drums! He'll go mad! Hurry up!" Nyakweleka herself, not a man, sang for Sakweleka [i.e., conducted a ritual for him]. At dawn, she filled his *lipele* with pieces of bark. These were his first *jipelo*.

Sakweleka threw out Nyakweleka's pestle, saying it had become powerless. He began divining with his *lipele*. But he shared his gains with Nyakweleka, in the same way that today a diviner shares his gains with Nyaminenge. Thus they continued for a long time, Sakweleka divining with the *lipele*, and Nyakweleka taking her share of the divination payments to her relatives, and giving Sakweleka food to eat.

When Nyakweleka died, Sakweleka asked her relatives what he should do with his oracle. He laid the *lipele* and all the marriage possessions on the ground and said, "I've bore children with Nyakweleka. I'll make a living with this oracle and look after Nyakweleka's children." They agreed. Sakweleka divined in their land, among the Lunda, for a long time; then, he returned to his village. This is how we Luvale received the *lipele*. The bow belonged to a woman, but a man took it from her. At Nyakapamba Musopa, Mwachiyavwa, Nyakweleka divined with a pestle. These are my words about Nyakweleka.

From an academic, chronology-based understanding of history, this divinatory epic is highly anachronistic. Western historians have dated the departure of Chinyama from Musumba in the late 1400s, and the creation of the Lunda Empire in about 1700 (Papstein 1978:43, Vellut 1972:68). If, as several diviners told me, Nyakweleka and Sakweleka lived long before Luweji married Ilunga, they could not possibly have been Luvale or Lunda, ethnicities that would emerge later. But the diviners, of course, were not wrong, because their intention lay not in chronology but in analogy: Nyakweleka lost her divinatory tool to Sakweleka in the same way that Luweji lost her royal insignia to Ilunga. Similarly, countess basket makers have lost their baskets to the diviners who commissioned them. Pezo lost her basket to diviner Sakutemba on 17 October 1996. This transfer of power from women to men pervades ritual and political life in the Upper Zambezi, being encapsulated in a famous Luvale proverb: *Uta wapwile wapwevo lunga amunyangawo* (The bow belonged to a woman and was taken from her by a man).

No diviner ever spelled out these correspondences for me, but the ethnography speaks for itself. In oral history and ritual action alike, the theme of the transfer of power from women to men is everywhere, echoing the structural tension between male authority and matriliny. No wonder then that this transfer of power is described as the stealing of a "bow," a powerful and productive object.

Hence it is that basket diviners are all men. Sangombe said that the number of *lipele* multiplied among Sakweleka's kin, the Luvale, and all the others whom they married and lived with, although he could not recall any individual names. All he knew was that the *lipele* "spread" across the region as Kayongo, the divinatory spirit, seized new men. As people left Musumba and migrated elsewhere, Kayongo followed them. In the case of the Luvale (here

Sangombe is no longer speaking), Kayongo embarked on a voyage of approx-
imately 1,000 kilometers, as Chinyama and his descendants marched down
the Lulua River, veered toward the Kasai, crossed the Luena and then the
Lumbala, onward to the Lungwebungu. On this southward route, Chinyama's
descendants mixed with groups of Mbwela in the Upper Zambezi, thus creating the Luvale ethnicity (Papstein 1978). The Atlantic trade began and ended,
colonialism came and went, and the civil wars swept Angola. Yet Kayongo
is still active, unshaken by the winds of change and the turbulence of social
havoc. Today, centuries after Sakweleka became the first *lipele* diviner, basket
divination is practiced in the vast area where Zambia, Angola, and the Democratic Republic of the Congo share borders, an area of no less than 700,000
square kilometers, and among such diverse groups as the Luvale, Chokwe,
Luchazi, Mbunda, Ndembu, Lunda-Shinde, Minungu, Ovimbundu, Songo,
Lwimbi, and Nyemba.

Lihamba Kayongo

It is not easy to grasp who or what Kayongo is. I came to see him (Kayongo
is perceived as male) as an energy field that collapses and reconfigures the
boundaries between objects and subjects. I do not mean to say that at some
point in their biographies things can become persons, and persons, things,
which they certainly can and do; I mean rather that the ontological states of
personhood and thingness are intentionally destabilized and dissolved within
ritual in order to achieve purposeful transformation. This is how I came to
see Kayongo, not how Kayongo was described to me.

I was often told that Kayongo is a spiritual manifestation of named dead
diviners. To say that a particular male ancestor or that Kayongo is afflicting
someone is one and the same thing. Yet the fact that all these dead diviners
manifest themselves as Kayongo suggests that they are the means through
which Kayongo, a male entity endowed with personality and volition, persists. In the Luvale language, this and many other manifestations of the dead
are known as *mahamba vausoko* (kinship *mahamba*); they afflict their living
kin with illness, reproductive disorders, and bad luck in hunting if hatred
and conflict arise in the villages, or if the living forget their predecessors and
fail to continue their professions. Kayongo is a *lihamba* (singular of *mahamba*) that runs in the families of diviners.[5]

A man caught by Kayongo becomes ill. People say that Kayongo has
seized him (*namukwate*) or made him stumble (*namulimbula*), forcing him

to become a diviner. People know that Kayongo, in addition to being violent, cruel, and altogether indifferent to the suffering wrought by historical contingency, is notoriously stubborn, so many songs are sung, drums played without rest, and substances repeatedly manipulated in an attempt to appease him during ritual. When at last the man's body begins to jerk and produce a deep guttural sound, the collective sentiment among the ritual participants is one of relief. Kayongo has conceded to "emerge" (*kulovoka*) or "rise" (*kukatuka*). The possessed man has been emptied of his subjectivity and turned into a vessel for Kayongo, a mere object.

Sakutemba once told me that Kayongo is like the wind. Most of the time we do not notice the wind; but when it gains velocity and momentum, we can hear it and feel it. Who has ever seen Kayongo making a man stumble or whispering the right answers in the diviner's ear? Kayongo dwells in a world that is inaccessible to the human senses. Most of the time, quietly and imperceptibly, from afar, he watches the behavior of his living relatives; then, all of a sudden, he makes someone stumble.

Kayongo also manifests itself in less violent ways that do not make the diviners ill or throw them into "possession trance" (Boddy 1994:407, 1989). At a divination session, for example, Kayongo communicates with the diviner by means of material *jipelo* configurations and short episodes of needle pricking in the diviner's heart, reportedly painful but tolerable. The pricking in the heart tells the diviner that he has found the right answer to his question in the form of a *jipelo* configuration; he translates what he sees to his clients, and the pain subsides.

Thus Kayongo belongs as much to the ethereal world of the ancestors as to the embodied world of the living. The sound of special rattles, the diviner's invocation, certain songs, drumbeats, and medicines entice him to come out. It is also said that Kayongo is a red *lihamba* that both heals and kills, both exposes evildoers and has a foot in their world. Like ambivalence itself, Kayongo is red; and so are many of his elements: red clay, blood, the bloodwood tree, the lourie's wing feathers, the red-necked francolin, the red mongoose.

Sakutemba's Predicament

Diviner Sakutemba told me how he came upon Kayongo. Sometime in his twenties, not long after his arrival in Chavuma from Angola, I surmised, he became ill with chronic headaches, sharp pains in his chest, fever, visual disturbances, and occasional signs of lunacy. These symptoms persisted for several months, so his father decided to consult the *lipele* of diviner Chilonga, an Angolan who would die in Zambia. It turned out that a matrilineal ancestor of Sakutemba who had been a basket diviner during his lifetime wanted Sakutemba to continue his profession. In the 1990s, afraid to disclose his Angolan identity, Sakutemba described this ancestor as a distant, classificatory grandfather whom he had never known, a Zambian-born man named Sachala who had died in Mize, near the Zambian township of Zambezi. On my return to Chavuma in 2002, just a few months after the signing of the peace accord in Angola, however, Sakutemba made it a point to clarify that this ancestor had in reality been his mother's full brother Muchivi, a man whom Sakutemba had known well. Together, they had walked all the way from Angola to escape the military confrontations of the liberation struggle in 1966.

Sakutemba did not welcome the news that his ancestor wanted him to become a diviner. Life in Chavuma was lived in poverty and fear, but he had found happiness. A smile on his face, he shared in reminiscence that he had spent his youth frolicking in the neighborhood, meeting girls in the bush, dancing *shombe*, and accompanying the men to the fishing camps at the onset of the cold weather. He knew how to farm, how to fish with long *makinda* traps in the flooded plains, how to forge iron blades for hoes, axes, spears, arrows, and knives. He also knew how to cure insanity, women's sterility, children's epilepsy, and even witchcraft-related conditions, although he found healing a bit of a nuisance, the patient paying the doctor only upon recovery. All in all, despite the wounds of forced displacement and resettlement, he had no reason to complain. Now his ancestor wanted him to become a diviner. To lift his spirits, he reminded himself that sometimes Kayongo releases his prey; women, he said, may suffer from Kayongo, but it is their male relatives who become *lipele* diviners. He was no woman most certainly, but weren't some men afflicted by benevolent Kayongo manifestations whose only expectation was to be honored in a nightlong ceremony?

After consulting Chilonga's *lipele*, Sakutemba's father asked the late Angolan diviner Kakwaya to conduct a nightlong ritual for propitiating Kayongo, hence curing Sakutemba. Meanwhile, because Sakutemba's maternal predecessors had buried the *lipele* of their dead relative at the riverside following his burial, a new basket was commissioned.

A month later, following the nightlong healing ceremony and a short period of seclusion inside his house, Sakutemba set off to Kamisamba, Chavuma, to "steal" the basket from the late basket maker Nyachinyama. In preparation for the coming ceremony of filling the new basket, he acquired a billy goat, a red cockerel, and plenty of bulrush millet beer. He also apprenticed himself to diviner Kakwaya, an experience that changed his view of the divinatory profession. Noticing the heavy payments and the deference that his master inspired in others, he began to think that basket divination suited him well after all. There was a double meaning in being seized by an ancestor: in the first, one was punished, made ill, stripped of one's autonomy, forced to become something previously inconceivable and unwanted; in the second, once the ancestral manifestation had been placated and controlled, one found himself with a tutelary spirit who confers health, curative powers, and divinatory knowledge.

In passing, this is true for other individuals who become specialized healers through affliction, as Turner notes for the Ndembu (1967:10, 1968). I. M. Lewis says of the "shaman" that he is both possessed by the spirit and in possession of the spirit (1971:47-50, 170-72). The relationship between Kayongo and the diviner is equally ambiguous.

Yet years of divination practice had changed little in Sakutemba's life. Did not his many skills suggest that God had destined him for glory? When we met in 1996 he seemed to see himself as a lesser person. Mindful that not everything in his life could be explained by the troubles caused by forced displacement, he once compared himself to diviner Sanjamba from Chilyakawa, an Angolan whom he saw as a picture of success. He, on the contrary, lived with one wife and his children under a thatched roof half-eaten by termites, and only Pili, his nephew and divination apprentice, had cared to settle in his village. This village had once belonged to his late father. His matrilineal relatives—a classificatory mother (his mother's full sister) and her daughter— resided in the village of Sakutemba's late maternal uncle.

With only one wife and a small, dilapidated village, the only signs of Sakutemba's accomplishments as a diviner were his divination symbols proper—two grayish pointed poles with an approximate height of thirty centimeters, known as *minenge*. Like the tiny wooden figures contained in the *lipele*, such poles are carved out of *mukula* (*Ptecarpus angolensis* [Horton 1953:139]). This tree is sometimes designated in English as "bloodwood" because of the crimson, resinous gum it oozes when cut. Diviners often color their *minenge* poles with red and white horizontal stripes. Sakutemba, however, had neglected to paint his poles, for Kayongo, he told me playfully, would not mind.

Beside the *minenge* poles were two light-barked trees known as *miyombo* (plural of *muyombo*, or *Lannea stuhlmanni* [White 1961:6]), today rarely

12. *Minenge* poles painted with red and white stripes (Sangombe's village, Chavuma, 1999; photo by author)

seen in Chavuma. These serve as central shrines in ceremonies that transfer the names and *lukano* bracelets of praised ancestors to their living relatives. One of Sakutemba's *miyombo* consisted of a sapling planted for Mushivi, his matrilineal ancestor who had seized him in the form of Kayongo; the other, a fully grown tree, had been set up decades earlier by Sakutemba's patrilateral relatives upon resettlement in Chavuma. Unlike the bloodwood poles, which dry up, decay, and need replacement, *miyombo* strike from cuttings and grow into light-crowned trees.

In moments of pessimism, Sakutemba thought of abandoning the arts of healing and divination and of dedicating himself full-time to fishing and cultivating. But he knew that this was only a reverie. The day he quit his profession, his ancestor would punish him with disease. In other moments, however, suggesting that he reconciled himself with this relationship and lifelong commitment, Sakutemba attempted to make the best of what he had been given and could not give back.

He had, for example, refused the title of Nyaminenge (The-Mother-of-the-Minenge) to his wife, in effect depriving her of an important source of wealth and prestige. Typically, Nyaminenge is responsible for looking after the *lipele* at home, where it is usually kept unless in use. As her relationship with the oracle "places her apart" (Nyaminenge *ajilila ngombo*), she must follow certain pre-scriptions and avoidances lest the oracle become powerless. His wife, however, Sakutemba told me bluntly, had broken the taboo against committing "adultery in daytime" (*ujila wamusana*) more than once. She was a good wife overall, hardworking and fertile, but her penchant for love affairs threatened his *lipele*.

Sakutemba also hoped to become wealthier by improving his divinatory tools. He was a *mukakutaha wavivimbi*, a diviner who can divine the causes of death, and no mere *mukakutaha wakalya pemba,* a diviner whose exper-tise is limited to cases of disease, infertility, and bad luck in hunting, cases that in 1996 yielded at the most 10,000 *kwachas*. A case of death yielded a bovine animal or the equivalent in cash, about 100,000 *kwachas* (100 US dol-lars). So Sakutemba took what he saw as the necessary steps to attract more clients and more cases of death. First, he looked for two powerful substances that were missing in his *jisomo* horns: a luring composite charm known as *tambikila* (*tambikila*, from *kutambika*, to call out, is also the name of a bird with an enticing call) (Horton 1953:381) and a scarlet feather from the tail or undertail coverts of the grey parrot, *kalongo* (*Psittacus erithacus* [Horton 1953:187]). These substances are said to attract clients and bring fame to the diviner. Second, he decided to commission a new *lipele*. When, as described in Chapter 1, I suggested that he order the basket from Pezo, he gladly acqui-esced. We agreed that I would pay for the basket making and cover the expenses incurred with the basket's ritual consecration. I would purchase a billy goat, a red cockerel, alcoholic beverages, and food for the meals. I would also give Sakutemba 2,000 *kwachas* for the diviner conducting the nightlong ceremony. Sakutemba, on his side, would ask his wife and relatives to brew bulrush millet beer and prepare food for the ritual participants; he would pay the hired diviner when the new basket produced wealth; and, of course, he would choose and invite that diviner in person. I had feared that Sakutemba would invite his "divination friend" Sanjamba, who lived nearby; but he chose instead Sangombe, an Angolan diviner from Kusongo, Chavuma, because they were "related through the oracle" (*usoko wangombo*) in addition to being "divination friends"; that is, the basket of diviner Kakwaya, who had filled Sakutemba's first basket, had been filled by the same man who had also filled Sangombe's first basket.

Sakutemba hoped that this closer relationship would make Sangombe less unyielding and materialistic. I too nourished this hope, for I wished to tape-record and photograph part of the nightlong ceremony. Though my own discomfort with flash photography would keep the snapping to a minimum,

13. Diviner Sangombe (Chavuma, 2002; photo by author)

Sangombe had the right and power to refuse my request, as other diviners had done. To my relief, however, he posed no obstacles.

Equally important, Sakutemba would ensure that a reasonable number of experienced people came to "help" him with the *lipele* ceremony. For the Angolans residing in Chavuma, whose families had been forced to disperse and resettle in different parts of Zambia, from Chavuma to the official refugee settlement in Meheba, near Solwezi, the number of such "helpers" always became a source of worry and concern. A low number of attendees not only would visibly index the low social status and prestige of the ritual subjects but also would threaten the efficacy of the ritual performance. Rituals, as Tambiah has shown, may be valid intrinsically, their acts being "constitutive" in the sense that their "very performance achieves the realization of the performative effect" (1979:128); yet they require performers in both the numerical sense and the qualitative sense of skilled performers. Nightlong ceremonies require a set of skilled "helpers."

Consider the drummers (always men) and the singers (mostly women). Their "help" is critical because a nightlong ritual is a very long act of singing and drumming, occasionally accompanied by some dancing or interrupted for a rest. Nightlong rituals without singing and drumming are not nightlong rituals, and it is no coincidence that the expressions *kumwimbila* (singing for someone) and *kumwimbila ngoma* (drumming for someone) stand metaphorically for their performance. It is true that singing and drumming through the night can lead to tedium, monotony, sleepiness, and even distancing. Yet repetition and redundancy are integral to the telic structure of rituals because they facilitate the easy recognition of patterns and configurations without which aesthetic enjoyment—and the ability to sing and drum until the morning—would be impossible (Tambiah 1979).

Singing is critical in another way. Amid all songs selected freely from the cultural repertoire during a *lipele* initiation ritual, a group of them must be sung in a fixed order. These songs give a sense of direction and purpose to the ritual, allowing the participants to orient themselves in the sequence that will lead to the consecration of the *lipele*. Not only do their lyrics describe important ritual actions, such as cutting medicines or filling the *lipele*, but they are also the verbal component of such actions, being sung while certain movements are performed and substances manipulated. In addition to being descriptive or propositional, they *do* something.[6] I have capitalized the titles of this group of songs in the following ethnographic description.

Sangombe Fills Sakutemba's Basket

17 October 1996

7:00 P.M.

After a strenuous bicycle ride on sand and rock in the dark, Cedric, my research assistant, and I made it to Sakutemba's village plaza in Kalwiji. Two open fires raged in the dark, and the smell of burning wood filled the air. Three women were cooking inside a round kitchen hut. A handful of men were conversing in the *zango*, a thatched structure where men gather. A mob of children ran wildly in all directions. Lying on the ground by the *minenge* poles and the *miyombo* trees, several objects revealed the type of ceremony that was about to begin: an old *lipele*; a new *lipele* wrapped with a plastic bag; a *kumba* basket, used for carrying the *lipele* and its paraphernalia; two *jisomo* horns; an iron *lilunge* bell; a two-calabash xylophone; a goatskin; and an arrow.

I sat on a blue sofa chair next to my neighbor Sambongo, a convivial middle-aged man who liked to portray himself as a Luvale from Chavuma, even though his fluent Portuguese and facial scarification marks, typical of the Songo people in Angola, left no room for doubt. Sambongo had come to the ceremony to sell cigarettes.

As soon as I sat down, Sakutemba emerged from the men's *zango*. Squatting by my legs, he politely informed me that the bundle of food that I had purchased for the ceremony was too small and that Sangombe, the diviner invited to direct the ceremony, expected a final payment of 50,000 *kwachas* to be delivered in the morning. Sakutemba assured me that Sangombe would not be willing to lower the price, however closely related they were. We discussed the matter for a short while, and I ended by agreeing to give him more food and an initial sum of 5,000 *kwachas*. He thanked me and walked away.

I noticed that a small group of Sakutemba's relatives, friends, and neighbors had now joined us around the largest open fire, the men sitting on chairs and small stools on one side, and the women and children sitting on mats and *vitenge* cloths on the other side. I had been offered a sofa chair among the men even though I am a woman because of my visitor status and identity—white women sit on chairs and stools, like men. While three drummers were tying tall drums to their waists, Pili (Sakutemba's nephew) began to play the xylophone. Diviner Sangombe joined in with the *lusangu* rattle. Clad in gray cotton pants, an orange sweater, and a Syracuse University baseball hat, he appeared younger than usual and oddly North American. Behind the chairs, stools, and mats, a crowd of people from nearby villages gathered.

9:00 P.M.

The drumming began. Sakutemba emerged from his house, wearing a depersonalizing loincloth known as *mulamba* over a ragged pair of shorts. He sat on a tiny wooden stool right in front of the drums, facing east, while his classificatory sister, a young woman named Sombo, carried a big metallic pot, a smaller pot, and a large calabash closed with leaves of *muvangwa* (*Paropsia brazzeana* [White 1961:1]), all of which she laid on the ground by the fire. As Sombo carried her load, Sangombe and the ritual participants sang a Chokwe song: *Pekama meya, mbunge yami tekuma* (BRING THE WATER, MY HEART IS THROBBING). The chorus soon lapsed into silence, as Sangombe, holding a root from the *muhuhu* tree (*Combretum spp.* [White 1959:1]), softly invoked his Angolan predecessors who had passed down the *lipele* to him.

Sangombe, later (explaining the ritual retrospectively), said:

First we invoke the women. Nyakweleka was the first diviner, and Semi and Mumba came from the east. The bow belonged to a woman before a man took it from her. During the invocation we say, "Quick quick quick, one must be taught the right medicines by an expert,

Ngombo yalya matemo yalya mazembe [The oracle eats hoes and eats axes]. This is how the medicines are received. I invoke my predecessors by saying, "I received my medicines from Litwayi, my mother's brother, and Litwayi received them from Chikumi. We all received the medicines thanks to our possessions [*vikumba*]. We gave a big black ox. You died, Litwayi, and I'm your successor, the holder of the *mutungu* [container in which medicines are kept, here the *lipele*] you once held; I have replaced you. Now, let *lihamba* Kayongo emerge quickly." This is how the invoking goes.

Sangombe announced that the goal of the ceremony was to replace an old *lipele* with a new one, not to initiate a man into divination, for Sakutemba had been a diviner for decades. Several times in his speech he referred to himself as "the owner of the tails," a direct reference to the Luvale riddle *Soko mukila, hundu mukila, mwenya mukila hiya?* (The vervet monkey has a tail, the yellow baboon has a tail, who is the owner of the tails?)[7] The monkey and baboon represent two different diviners, and their tails represent the diviners' baskets. By describing himself as the owner of the tails, Sangombe underscored his professional seniority to Sakutemba and the other diviners whose baskets he had filled.

Sangombe axed a *muhuhu* root on a thick log, as the crowd sang in unison, *Teta vitumbo* (CUT THE MEDICINES). He tossed thick root slices into the big metallic pot and added other root medicines: small pieces of root from the *katwaumbwangu* tree and the *musole* tree (*Vangueriopsis lancifora* [Horton 1953:355]), a larger piece of bloodwood root, and a root from a tree stump found in the plains. This tree was said to have lost its crown to the wind, much like the dead diviner lost his *lipele* to death.

Sangombe, later repeating the words he had used to address the stump in the plains, said, "'My predecessor, to whom have you left your oracle? You have no crown. Today, I've come to collect a root from you, a tree without crown. You're dead, headman, and I'll collect my root. Let my medicines cure people, let my medicines attract Kayongo. If you, Kayongo, are a delusion produced by witches and wizards, a mere illusion, do not emerge; if you are the real Kayongo, emerge then, let everyone see you.' This is how it goes."

A woman pounded leaf-medicine in a mortar near the *minenge* poles. These leaves came from the same trees as the roots that were sliced and tossed into the pot. The "leaves from above" ended inside the mortar, and the "roots from below" ended inside the pot. The pounding accompanied the

song *Twenu vitumbo* (POUND THE MEDICINES), which soon drifted into
another song with the same drum and bell rhythms:

> Ndo! Ndo! Doing what?
> Pounding.
> Who pounded the medicines?
> What was pounded?
> A tree stump in the path
> What was pounded?
> Hurt ten toes.[8]
> What was pounded?
> The red-necked francolin [*ngwali*][9]
> What was pounded?
> The red skin of the mongoose [*mukondo*].[10]
> What was pounded?

As the crowd began to chant another song, *Longa vitumbo* (FILL WITH
MEDICINES), Sangombe placed the big metallic pot on his and Sakutemba's
feet, and added more roots and the leaf-medicine pounded in the mortar.
Had he filled the pot on the ground, so it is said, the *lipele* would have become
powerless or, in Sangombe's evocative wording, "a mere vessel for the bed-
bugs to lay their eggs." A few people tossed more medicines into the pot, as
later in the ritual they would toss *jipelo* into the basket.

Sangombe removed the leaf lid from the calabash. He called out to the
witches and wizards who might have wished to disturb the ceremony: "May
the witches and wizards [*vakashili vaze vakakulova*] come and end on the
muvangwa leaves! May the ones on this side come and take some leaves, may
the ones on the other side come and take some leaves, too!" He held the calabash and poured some water behind and in front of the big and small metallic
pots. He added the remaining water to the medicines. Then Sangombe continued: "May those nursing ill feelings [*shili*] land on the leaves and depart with
them! The witches and wizards are responsible for their own acts of witchcraft.
You staying in the East, you in the West, you in the North, you in the South,
take the leaves I address in your direction, know that the things finishing your
village are your own doing." Sangombe pinched some red clay from a small
leather pouch and spread it over the fire while saying, "You, witch, may your
anus burn in the fire." He placed the big pot on the fire and sunk a splashing
broom (*chisapo*) inside for a few minutes. This broom is made of *chikanga-
lwiji* grass. The same grass is used for making the belts seen on the corpse of

diviners, one around the waist, and the other over one shoulder. As the herbal solution boiled, everyone sang *Teleka ndeho* (COOK POT).

In the eventuality that Sakutemba died unexpectedly during the ceremony, Sangombe drank a sip of medicine from the small pot as proof that it was not poisonous. Only then, his back turned to Sakutemba, did he pass the pot to him, as the ritual participants sang *Nwisa vitumbo* (MAKE HIM DRINK THE MEDICINE).

Following Sangombe's directive, Sakutemba mechanically squatted on the ground and leaned over the big pot, now lying by the *minenge* poles. The steam from that pot is said to remove the "blur" from the diviner's eyes, enabling him to see the things of the night—the eyes of diviners are able to see things that ordinary eyes, being "blurred," cannot see. Sangombe covered Sakutemba and the pot with a blanket. Everyone sang *Fwika vitumbo* (COVER THE MEDICINES) for as long as Sangombe shook the *musambo* rattle above the blanket.

Then Sangombe lifted the blanket, cueing the crowd to sing *Kombela nganga* (DO THE INVOCATION, DOCTOR), which he did in the way previously described. He soaked the splashing broom both in the big pot and in the mortar, and he hit it lightly on Sakutemba's back, chest, and head. He splashed his whole body (*kusapwila*). The leaf and root medicine is said to attract Kayongo. Sangombe also splashed Sakutemba's goatskin and the new *lipele* as he pointed them in the cardinal directions.

10:00 P.M.

At the first signs of *lihamba* activity, the crowd clustered around Sakutemba. The pace of splashing increased, the drumming became more vibrant, and the singing louder. Soon Sakutemba's body began to jerk and twitch (*kutunguta*) while producing a hoarse sound. (People describe *mahamba* vocalizations in general by means of the triple sound sequence "Hoho! Hoho! Hoho!") In the seated position, legs clamped like pliers onto the small stool, Sakutemba's body sprung repeatedly about one meter above the ground and darted off through the thicket of people. A group of men ran after Sakutemba. That was Ngungu, a very violent *lihamba* that likes the bush. Had the men not caught Sakutemba in the surrounding maize fields and brought him back to the village, he would have possibly fled to the bush and gone mad. Sangombe rubbed some medicines on Sakutemba's face to calm Ngungu down. Exhausted and beaten, Sakutemba returned to the wooden stool.

Ngungu, like Kazanga, is a *lihamba* that belongs with the boys' initiation ceremony (*mukanda*). I learned later that Sakutemba had received Ngungu from a maternal ancestor who had been *mukafunda*, a ritual expert who is responsible for protecting the initiates against evildoers. Ngungu is not a divination *lihamba*. I was told that Ngungu often emerges during divination ceremonies because he cannot resist the call of the beautiful Kayongo drumming and singing.

One more session of splashing, singing, and drumming, and Kayongo finally emerged. This time Sakutemba's body jerked slowly and gently. Kayongo seemed surprisingly calmer than Ngungu. A bit of medicine rubbed on Sakutemba's face was all it took to calm down this *lihamba*. The ritual had now reached its first pinnacle, and the crowd looked forward to a rest.

Back in their seats, the women challenged one another to sing. A brief moment of rehearsal preceded each new song, as the drummers strove to synchronize with the fervent singers. Three women jumped to their feet and began to dance near the larger open fire. They were Sakutemba's relatives from a nearby village, he told me proudly. Pili joined the women. They teased one another with swift hip shakes that contrasted gracefully with the slow, elegant movement of their arms and hands. Pili danced to the *kachacha* dance song *Chikungulu naMundenda*, his long white shirt waving and flickering in the dark.

Chikungulu naMundenda tunavawane	Chikungulu and Mundenda, we've met them
Kufwane nafu Ngwele nashiki ngwenyi	If I die, said Ngwele
Vano vanyike muvalama	Look after my children

Chikungulu and Mundenda were two celebrated MPLA fighters during the Angolan civil wars. Ngwele was a pastor at the Chavuma Mission. In 1988, when Ngwele's brother died unexpectedly, his relatives took the case to diviner Sanjamba, who accused Ngwele of being a wizard. Shocked and enraged, they darted back to their village. They stoned Ngwele to death and burned his body. On hearing the revengeful crowd approaching the village, Ngwele's son had run to his father and urged him to escape into the bush. But Ngwele had refused. He had calmly grabbed his spear and sat down in the men's shelter, waiting.

11:00 P.M.

Sangombe, Sakutemba, Pili, and Cedric gathered in Sakutemba's house to smoke cigarettes and drink the alcoholic beverages that I had purchased for the occasion: tea wine and a distilled booze called *lituku*. There was no bulrush millet beer because Sakutemba's wife, having been denied the status of Nyaminenge, had refused to brew it. The four men remained indoors for two hours. By the time they came outside, the number of participants had dropped to about thirty. Except for Sambongo, the cigarette seller, all those who were not connected to Sakutemba through ties of kinship, vicinity, or close friendship had left. Their excitement about seeing a ritual rarely performed had quickly subsided at the dismal prospect of staying awake all night with a dry throat. Conversations with Sakutemba prior to the ritual had led me to expect a small attendance, but I could sense the collective feeling of disappointment. Sambongo blamed it on Chavuma, possibly betraying memories of better-attended rituals in Angola.

Following a few laudatory words about my interest in the Luvale tradition, Sangombe stood up and said solemnly:

> For those of you who have come to help, Sakutemba will reduce the divination price when you consult his new *lipele*. For those who have already left, he will do the opposite. [At this point, Sangombe sang the song *Talila kumeso mukandumba wazangama* (Look into the eyes, the witch is smart).] When you kill a snake and people come to help you skinning it, notice the ones who spit to the side; do not share your snake with them. As the proverb goes, *Vatu naulya navo noka, nautalila kukuva* [Before sharing your snake with others, remember the skinning]. When you cut down a *mupafu* tree and people come to help you collecting the *jipafu* fruits, notice the ones who selfishly pile up the fruits in their heaps—do not eat with them. I cannot hide. *Ami kusaza kushikila kuhanjika kulumbununa* [Vomiting covers up, talking uncovers the truth]. *Ngwapwa ngumupandu waTumba, kupandumuna hikuhana* [I am Mupandu waTumba (Mupandu derives from *kupandumuna*, or to uncover), I uncover the truth and give it to you]. Though I am a small mannikin, I fly beside the big birds, carrying twigs to the nest.[11]

As soon as Sangombe sat down, closing his speech, Pili announced that six bottles of the distilled booze had been saved for those who had come to aid Sakutemba; no booze for the selfish, he said scornfully. Pili's mimicking of the clumsy movements of a drunkard made us all laugh.

Sangombe splashed more medicine on Sakutemba. The chorus incited Sangombe to dance by singing the song *Twaya utale omu alenga chimbanda*

(COME AND SEE HOW THE DOCTOR DANCES). The aim of this dance is to request gifts and remuneration (*jinyembu*) from the participants. A woman tied a *chitenge* cloth around Sangombe's waist to accentuate his hip movements, but after a few uninspired steps Sangombe refused to dance. He said that he could not "dance," meaning to request remuneration, because Sakutemba was "related" to him. Instead, he splashed the old and new divination baskets as he pointed them in the four directions and mercilessly cursed humanity:

Sangombe, later, said:

> May people fall sick, may people die all around me. A diviner is like the tiller who wishes hunger to the other tillers while he works hard on his field. If only he cultivates, he'll become wealthy by selling *shima* to them. Over there, in the direction I'm pointing this oracle, may people fall sick and consult my oracle, because I want their coins! I shake the basket in a different direction. You living in the East, break your head [*kupulika mutwe* stands for the various problems that lead to consulting a diviner], come to my oracle, for I crave your money! May someone die in Angola, so they rush to me with their money! People kill one another and come to consult me; I expose the witch or wizard who killed their relative; they pay me; then, they go back home and kill someone else. Crack your head! Die! Come here! I put the *lipele* down.

Then Sangombe faced eastward and quickly invoked Semi (The-Woman-with-Children) and Mumba (The-Childless-Woman), who came from the east, Semi smiling and Mumba weeping (*Hacheza hejile Semi naMumba, Semi hikwiza nakuseha, Mumba hikwiza nakulila*).[12] He also invoked Nyakapamba Musopa from Musumba. He concluded by saying, "A woman owned the bow but a man took it from her."

The next two hours were filled with songs and dance. Only occasionally did Sangombe splash Sakutemba, who remained stone still on the wooden stool.

Emptying the Old Lipele

3:00 A.M.

Sangombe sank the new *lipele* into the big pot, now lying on the fire. A moment later, he removed it and bent it inward to reshape it. He walked to the *minenge* area and poured the *jipelo* from the old *lipele* onto the goatskin lying on the ground, all the while singing *Nanguzukula ngombo* (I'LL EMPTY THE ORACLE).

Then Sangombe returned to the large open fire, carrying the new and old baskets on top of each other, a reddish mongoose skin between them. He splashed medicine on both baskets and danced with them. He took the old basket back to the *minenge* area and came back to splash the new one a bit more and dance with it, as he said, "My first wife is now old and worn out, so she has to go. I've married a new wife, she is young, and she is the one I like. She cost me a hoe [meaning the traditional bride-price]. The *jipelo* yearn for a new basket. The time to empty the old one has come. I will bury it atop a large anthill. Now I'm dancing with my favorite wife."

4:00 A.M.

Sangombe joined a handful of men who had gathered around the smaller open fire. Sakutemba remained motionless and expressionless on the wooden stool, seemingly indifferent to the moving songs. One song spoke of a dead girl named Kalumbu who is said to have appeared above the surface of a river in Angola to tell her tragic story. She had accompanied her grandmother to the riverside to collect a certain grass used for making *mukele* salt. It was there at the riverside that her grandmother chopped her neck with an axe.

Ou mwana mwaswita mukele wenyi	While cutting *mukele* grass
Weyenge weyenge	*Weyenge weyenge*
Ou Kalumbu kaLushiya	Kalumbu, Lushiya's daughter
Weyenge weyenge	*Weyenge weyenge*
Namuchache hashingo nahakota	Was chopped on the nape of the neck

The women also sang the cheerful popular song *Vanasavala vanasavala* (They are asleep, they are asleep), which the youth in Chavuma inevitably sing at *chikinya* dances:

Vanasavala vanasavala	They are asleep, they are asleep
Vakwetu vose vanasavala	They are all asleep
Yiye yiye	*Yiye yiye*

Sangombe returned to the main circle and splashed Sakutemba until his body became drenched in medicine. He swayed the mongoose skin above the fire in all directions. He went back to the *minenge* area, grabbed Sakutemba's

divining flask—a subsidiary oracle—from the *kumba* carrying basket, and
pointed it in the same directions that he had pointed the mongoose skin.

5:00 A.M.

"Hoho! Hoho! Hoho!" This time Kayongo made Sakutemba's body jerk in
furor. Kayongo took off to the *minenge* area and attacked the leg-tied billy
goat. Sangombe ran to cover the scene with a blanket. To help his uncle
slaughter the animal and cut its belly open, Pili crawled underneath. We
heard the goat bleating. A woman passed the red cockerel to them. As the
blanket wavered in midair I got a glimpse of Sakutemba, biting off the fowl's
neck with his teeth.

Goat and cockerel finally slaughtered, Sangombe removed the blanket.
The three men proceeded to pull out the old *minenge* poles. They filled one
of the small holes left on the ground with goat blood and the contents of the
goat's first stomach (*ufwachi*), and poked a new *munenge* pole in there. They
stuck the cock's head onto this pole's pointed end. Sangombe anointed both
the pole and Sakutemba's eyes with rooster and goat blood.

Sangombe, later, said:

> The diviner whose eyes were anointed with blood feels no pity. If his
> mother-in-law [with whom he has an avoidance relationship] kills his
> wife, he will feel no sympathy for her because his eyes were rubbed with
> blood, and the rooster's head was stuck onto the *munenge* pole. Staring
> at his mother-in-law in the face, he will say, "You have killed my wife!
> You own witchcraft familiars!" He will feel no shyness. He could say the
> same to his father-in-law, because his eyes were rubbed with the blood
> absorbed by the *munenge*. He resembles a bush; he is not shy. This is
> why we place the rooster's head on top of the *munenge*: it alerts us to the
> things of the night. Blood affects the pole; blood affects the *lipele*; blood
> affects the eyes. The diviner's eyes demand blood and red clay. His eyes
> are never white; his eyes are red. So you fear them. His eyes and the
> rooster's head are the same. This is how it goes.

Pili cut open the cockerel's chest and removed the heart. Sangombe stuck
a tiny piece from a broken needle and two thin chips shaved from a wooden
divination article (*kaponya*) into the fowl's heart, which he offered Sakutemba
to eat. "Swallow!" he said. The heart slid down Sakutemba's throat, but because
of the medicine he had drunk from the small pot, it stopped at his chest.

Sangombe, later, continued:

Each time a diviner defecates, he confirms that the needle is still inside his body. You might think that the needle will puncture his intestine walls, but no. You might say that it will come out while the diviner is squatting, but no. It's wedged in the rooster's heart. . . .

When the diviner gives the right answer to his clients, he feels his heart aching, Jo! Jo! Jo! He knows what is going on. Imagine that something is missing from a house. The woman tells the man that she can't find it; the man tells the woman that he hasn't touched it; so the woman suggests that they consult a *lipele*. The diviner shakes his basket. "You're a thief! You stole your wife's belongings!" He tells the man. He feels a sudden sharp pain in the heart, as if something has slit it open. He repeats, "You're a thief, don't deny it!" His heart is throbbing heavily. Then the man confesses, and the diviner's heart quiets down, mba mba mba. . . .

5:15 A.M.

Sangombe smeared the contents of the goat's first stomach on the inside and outside of the new *lipele*. This makes the basket stiff and heavy so that Sakutemba may shake it well. Once the *lipele* gained the right weight and firmness, Sangombe rubbed the goat's blood on the *lipele* and the *jipelo*, which were still lying on the goatskin by the *minenge*. He added a mix of red clay and castor oil to the basket.

Sangombe, later, said: "The red clay hides the basket's paleness. It hides that whiteness which the basket shows at birth. The red clay makes the basket red. When a diviner is shaking the *lipele*, the witches and wizards exclaim, '*Lipele!*' Everybody exclaims, '*Lipele!*' Because of its redness, we even forget the basket's initial appearance. This is the reason why we use red clay; it hides that whiteness. There is nothing else to it: no taboo [*chijila*] and no special power. Red clay is not medicine [*lupelo*]."

Once the *lipele* became stiff and red, Sangombe marked it on the inside with white clay and dressed it with three old animal skins, tightly fastening them with a rope around the rim. Between the rope and the rim he wedged an arrow. A broken arrow, or *mwivwi*, represents a pledge. It is used to seal the promise made by the living to their deceased relative that his or her death will be taken to a diviner. Transmuted into cash in today's monetized economy, it is also given by diviners as a deposit (*mwivi*) to the basket makers who coil their baskets.

14. The new *lipele*, rubbed with goat blood and the contents of the goat's stomach; two *somo* horns; two *minenge* poles, one topped with the rooster's head; and a two-calabash xylophone (Chavuma, 1996; photo by author)

Filling the New Lipele

6:00 A.M.

All the ritual participants followed the diviners to a nearby fork in the path. At the fork, Sangombe, Sakutemba, and Pili laid the old goatskin holding the *jipelo* on the ground and placed the new *lipele* on top. Each of them picked one divination article. Pili distributed the remaining articles among the crowd. I received the article Path, which I jokingly associated with my being in Chavuma. Playfully and wittily, Sakutemba responded that the article Path was as appropriate for a guest as his own article, Place, was appropriate for a host. We had a good chuckle.

The three men threw their *jipelo* into the new basket. We would have ruined Sakutemba's *lipele* had we thrown our articles first. Then, to the rhythm of the song *Kulonga ngombo* (FILL THE ORACLE), Sakutemba dragged the new *lipele* by the arrow down the sandy path leading to the village. We all followed behind, throwing our *jipelo* into the basket. We represented humanity, filling the basket with the tokens of human misery: evil agents, ill feelings, blameful conduct, disease, ill fortune, death. At one and the same time we were filling the basket that Sakutemba would use to divine the causes of

15. Tying an arrow onto the *lipele* at the fork in the path (Chavuma, 1996; photo by author)

16. Filling the *lipele* (Chavuma, 1996; photo by author)

suffering in 1990s Chavuma and reenacting the past ritual in which Nyak-weleka and Sakweleka had filled the original *lipele*.

Sangombe, later, described the act of filling the original basket: "Nyakweleka and Sakweleka filled the original *lipele* with roots, pieces of charcoal, animal parts, and other *jipelo*. Sakweleka carved small wooden figures. Upon noticing someone looking startled, they threw an article for the feeling of startledness [*ukasumuka*] into the basket. Someone stumbled on an ancestor-related affliction—they threw an article. Someone wailed for a deceased relative—they threw an article. A witch created a hyena familiar—they threw an article. All the *jipelo* in Nyakweleka's basket were assembled in this way."

By the time we reached the *minenge* poles, the basket had become an oracle. Famished dogs were licking blood off the ground. Sangombe grabbed the basket and shook it for the first time. He praised the quality of Pezo's work, for not a single article had flown out with the first shaking. Sangombe's work had been outstanding too, which led several people to step forward and drop small *kwacha* bills into the basket. Sakutemba contributed two bills of 500 *kwachas*. Sangombe stacked the bills, folded them gingerly, and tucked them into his pants pocket.

Sangombe rubbed white clay on Sakutemba's right arm. He wedged two *jisomo* horns into the eaves of Sakutemba's thatched roof (the word *somo*

17. Shaking the new *lipele* for the first time (Chavuma, 1996; photo by author)

derives from the verb *kusoma*, meaning "to insert"). These horns had been removed from reed-bucks found dead in the wild and were filled with powerful substances that attract new clients to the diviner.

Sangombe, later, described his use of *jisomo* horns:

Early in the morning, after people leave for the fields, I spit saliva on my *jisomo*. I look in all directions, in the same way that I pointed the *lipele* in all directions during the ceremony. In each direction, I mark the sand with the horn, twa! "You staying in Kalipande [Angola] break your head! Be bewitched! Come for divining and leave your coins with me!" Twa! "You living in Luyiland [Western Province, Zambia], kill your mother-in-law! Make your wife despise you, make her wish that I blame you for the death of her mother, allow me to eat your 1,000 *kwachas*." Twa! "You staying in Lumai [now Luvuei, Angola], crack your head!" Twa! "Crack your head! Let the sun burn you down—'Oh my head mama! Oh my head mama!'—run to my village so I will tell you the truth and anoint you with white clay." This white clay comes from the *lipele*. The *jisomo* horns are things of witchcraft and sorcery, like myself. This is how we work.

Having poked the *jisomo* horns into the eaves of Sakutemba's house, Sangombe walked to a nearby thicket to bury the splashing broom and empty the mortar and the big metallic pot. Sakutemba meanwhile had changed into ordinary clothing and was now sweeping the *minenge* area. At the women's request, I played back the tape that I had recorded during the night. They found it highly amusing to identify voices and distinct noises, such as a rooster crowing or the *jipelo* landing on the basket. As soon as I turned off the tape-recorder, Sangombe, now sitting cross-legged on a mat, called out: "Sakutemba! Give me my 50,000 *kwachas*!" He went on to explain that he deserved even a cow, for the *lipele* would attract many sufferers and much wealth to Sakutemba; but as he and Sakutemba were related as diviners, he was willing to lower the price. Sakutemba complained. "Fifty thousand *kwachas*! Aren't we related? Have I not cared to prepare good food?" Sangombe retorted that Sakutemba's food was stuck in his throat. He deserved to be paid for his work; Sakutemba must give him the money or he would remove the mongoose skin from the *lipele* and take it with him. Sakutemba rubbed his forehead on my arm, soliciting help. Fearing the worst, I gathered courage to intervene. But Sangombe cut me off by changing the course of the conversation. There was still work to be done, he said as he jumped to his feet.

Burying the Old Lipele

I followed Sangombe and Pili down a trail through thin bush. Sangombe carried the dead *lipele* on the palm of his left hand, as if holding a tray, and an axe on his left shoulder. Pili carried a bloodwood stick. We soon left the trail and headed to a gigantic anthill covered with thorny bushes. Pili buried the *lipele* on top of this anthill. He set up the bloodwood stick as a warning sign for women and children, for should they step over the grave, the *lipele*'s shadow (*muvwimbimbi*) would enter their bodies, making the children mad and the women bleed to death. Being associated with death and the underworld, an anthill is a perfect site for burying a *lipele*. Who within reason would climb an anthill? Other times, however, the *lipele* is buried at the riverside, another site associated with death, and an old, hardened stick (*sengwa*) is poked into the ground. This happens when a diviner dies with no descendant to inherit his *lipele*.

Back at the village, Sangombe summoned Sakutemba inside the house. I sat on the bright blue sofa chair next to my neighbor Sangombo, who was now wondering what to tell his wife when she asked him about the cigarette money. The night had been bad for business. When the two diviners returned outside,

Sakutemba came to rub his forehead on my arm. He needed my 5,000 *kwachas* and extra food before 10:00 a.m., at which time Sangombe would leave. So I tied my share of the sacrificed goat—one leg and the intestines—to my bicycle carrier, and rushed to the market.

The next day, the only sign that a *lipele* initiation ceremony had taken place at Sakutemba's village was the new *munenge* pole. Starving dogs had snatched the rooster's head from the pole's pointed end. Sakutemba had stored his new *lipele*, wrapped in animal skins, inside his *kumba* basket. On top of the skins he had placed his *lusangu* rattle, lourie's feather,[13] divining flask, *jisomo* horns, broken arrows, and *lilembu* (a tiny calabash bowl filled with medicine). Then he had covered the *kumba* basket with its lid and placed it on the goatskin, which now lay on top of a small stool located by the head of Sakutemba's bed.

Sakutemba reported that he gave Sangombe the bill of 5,000 *kwachas* and a tasty meal of dried fish cooked in tomatoes on his return. Some people had already come to consult him. He had welcomed them heartily, for their arrival had lifted the taboo on bathing and copulating, and, more importantly, had confirmed the power of the new *lipele* to attract people and wealth.

As for Sangombe, he had a different story to tell. He corroborated the clients' arrival and the closure of ritual avoidances, but he denied having eaten the food or received the money. As soon as my messenger had arrived with the parcel, he said, Sakutemba had grabbed it and "sneaked like a snake" into his house. Sakutemba's behavior had been "bitter like peppers," especially considering that Sangombe had given him his own *lipele* when Kayongo had initially caught Sakutemba. He knew from the start that no good would come of the ceremony. He had agreed to fill the new basket to shield himself from future false accusations, because, as he explained with a proverb, *Kasulu nahichi haunga, unga kumwangala chiku* (When a lizard passes over flour, the flour is not trashed). The wise think ahead.

I commented, dumbfounded, that Sakutemba had told me that he had been an apprentice to the late diviner Kakwaya and had commissioned his first *lipele* from the late basket maker Nyachinyama, as previously mentioned. Sangombe shook his head in disapproval. Sakutemba is a chameleon! he said. It was true that Sakutemba's relatives had consulted Kakwaya, who had pinned down an ancestor as the cause of Sakutemba's affliction. That said, Sangombe, and not Kakwaya, had initiated Sakutemba into divination. Driven by compassion and the duties toward a professional peer and a "divination relative,"

Sangombe had even offered Sakutemba his own *lipele* (the very basket we had buried on the anthill), knowing that the *lipele* of Sakutemba's ancestor had been buried at the riverside.

Thus we ended our conversation. I felt utterly confused with the names and events mentioned, and, although I knew that the widespread fear of further displacement to the refugee settlement in Meheba had probably led Sakutemba to rewrite history, I refrained from further inquiry.

A Way of Doing

Théodore Delachaux, a Swiss ethnographer who took part in the 1932–33 Swiss scientific expedition to Angola, once wrote: "The information on the baskets' consecration is rare and rather uneven; but it is certain that such consecration exists, showing the importance given to these recipients and the primary role they play in divination" (1946b:142; my translation from the French). Today, almost eighty years after the Swiss expedition, not much has been written about the basket itself apart from reporting its existence, naming it, and, in rare cases, identifying its weaving technique. Some authors have shown special interest in the intricate symbolism of the divinatory articles, whereas others have paid close attention to the diviner's first ritual of healing and invitation;[14] all in all, however, the information on the basket's consecration is still thin.

Here I wish to highlight the recurrent interest in the diviner's ritual of healing and initiation. It is true that this ritual is performed with the intention of curing the diviner and initiating him into divination, processes that in sub-Saharan Africa, as mentioned, are often mutually entailed. What is usually omitted, however, is the important fact that the same ritual complex that heals and initiates men may also initiate material objects. In the case of divination baskets commissioned and initiated as replacements for old, decrepit baskets, their initiation takes place long after that of their owners.

Note that the term *curative ritual* is here altogether inappropriate, as the diviner is not ill. It is preferable to speak of a life-crisis ritual that marks a crucial transition in the *lipele*'s lifetime, transforming a young, inexperienced basket into a mature oracle. Physically, its original "paleness" gives way to the brownish, slimy contents of the goat's first stomach, the reddish mix of castor oil and red clay, the white and red marks, the animal skins, and the divinatory articles. Socially, the *lipele* (and, through it, the diviner) enters a new human and material world. Hereafter it will serve as a container for the *jipelo* and stay in close association not only with other divinatory objects and substances—*minenge* poles, *jisomo* horns, *misambo* rattles, red clay and white chalk, blood, and so on—but also with people—mostly diviners, apprentices, vaNyaminenge, *lipele* weavers, and consulters. It will never feel the weight of flour or the touch of a woman's hands. The diviner, on his side, will expand his circle of (hopefully) dependable divination "friends" and "relatives"—a socially diverse circle that includes individuals from different families, clans, and even ethnicities—as well as his circle of lay dependents, from wives to relatives. As discussed in Chapter 1, divination brings wealth and prestige, which is the reason why the Angolan diviners who came to Chavuma as refugees did not take long to once again become persons.

Consecration

It is said that prior to consecration a *lipele* is a mere coiled basket, as worthless as a bedbug's nest. Or, in a more telling metaphor, a *lipele* with no diviner is a tree crown with no stump, a diviner with no *lipele* is a stump with no crown. A basket can only become an oracle if and when Kayongo intervenes.

How, then, is Kayongo enticed to the divination basket? Borrowing an expression from Luc de Heusch, I would say that Kayongo becomes "metonymically caught in a metaphorical trap" (1982, quoted in MacGaffey 1977:182). On the one hand, the senior diviner attracts Kayongo to the new *lipele* by transferring the articles from the old *lipele* into it. It is noteworthy that these articles are known in the Luvale language as *jipelo,* a term that conveys the idea of unseen powers inhering in matter, from its broader sense of organic substances used both to cure and to harm. In the same way that the singing of certain songs divides the ritual into temporal segments, the act of positioning *jipelo* divides the ritual into sequential parts: while the *jipelo* are inside the old basket; while the *jipelo* are on the goatskin (lest their life force dissipate into the ground); and while the *jipelo* are inside the new basket. It is to the actions behind these spatial and temporal configurations that Luvale speakers refer to when they wish to distinguish between the *lipele* initiation and other Kayongo rituals. A *lipele*'s initiation ritual is described as the ritual for "emptying the (old) oracle" (*kuzukula ngombo*), the ritual for "filling the (new) oracle" (*kulonga ngombo*), or the ritual for "making a transfer"(*kunungula*). The word *transfer* is used both in the physical sense that the *jipelo* of the old basket are moved into the new basket, and in the phenomenological sense that the new basket becomes the old one metonymically. The new basket becomes the baskets that preceded it and the late diviners who shook them, all of whom embodied Kayongo.

As happens in divination sessions, the *lipele* initiation pays homage to late persons and past events; it exhibits a "rhetoric of re-enactment," an overt willingness to continue the past that makes of it a commemorative event (Casey 1987:219-56, Connerton 1989:61).

Kayongo is also affixed to the *lipele* by means of its own metaphors. One way consists of inciting Kayongo to "come out" with such stimuli as words (invocations and songs), drumming, the shaking of rattles, and the splashing of herbal medicine on the *lipele* and the diviner's body. This medicine includes the roots and leaves from the same trees: the roots from below and the leaves from above. The roots represent a tree stump, a diviner without a *lipele*. The leaves represent the tree crown, a *lipele* without a diviner. By splashing leaf and root medicine on the *lipele*, the senior diviner animates it metaphorically. The basket becomes Kayongo. Concurrently, by splashing the same medicine on Sakutemba's body, the senior diviner incites Kayongo to emerge. Sakutemba becomes Kayongo. His personality, which the ritual systematically annuls by proscribing ordinary clothing and the expression of emotions and will, is now altogether absent. The Dinka of Sudan told Godfrey Lienhardt that during possession "they are literally 'not themselves'" (Lienhardt 1985:155). I think that the basket diviners would agree. Possession trance coincides with the de-possession of the self.

The personification of the *lipele* and the objectification of the diviner are therefore mutually entailed. Personification and objectification are inverse images of the same ontological continuum, a reality known to Luvale speakers as "Kayongo." In the process, the senior diviner unites the crown to the stump, the leaves to the roots, the above to the below.

I came to see Kayongo as sheer power and potentiality, a power that works by dissolving ontological boundaries between objects and subjects. When Kayongo possesses a man, this man goes into a possession trance, loses self-awareness, and becomes objectified. When Kayongo possesses a basket, this basket becomes an oracle, a personified object. All this in the hope that a man, diviner Sakutemba in this chapter, who saw himself as a lesser person compared to other diviners, may de-objectify himself. Prior to my fieldwork, I had been drawn to commoditization theory in part because it sees commoditization and de-commoditization as inverted expressions of the same continuum. Although the same principle of fluidity is central to *lipele* initiation, here it becomes expressed not as (de)commoditization, which is alien to it, but as ontological fluidity, ritual transformation, and existential rebirth.

But there is another way of attracting Kayongo with metaphor. Kayongo is described as a red *lihamba*, red being the color of its material symbols: the blood of the goat and the blood of the cockerel, the red clay, the rooster's feathers, the skin of the mongoose, the bloodwood tree latex. The senior diviner makes things red so that Kayongo comes out quickly.

We know from Victor Turner that red is the color of ambivalence in the red-white-black color classification of south Central Africa (1967/1965:59-92). Because in divination rituals the black color is absent, red assumes a myriad of negative meanings in conjunction with or in opposition to white. Hence the fact that the *lipele* is marked with red clay and white chalk, the *minenge* poles are often painted in red and white bands, and, in the past, on the occasion of a consultation into the cause of death, the diviners danced to the sound of divination songs, their bodies colored in red and white stripes (Baumann 1935:233, White 1948c:94).

On one side, in association with anthills and the underworld, red evokes death. We have seen that one burial site for dead divination baskets, signaled by a bloodwood pole, are thorny anthills; the other site is the riverside, which is also associated with death (White 1948b:29-30). The term *hungu*, meaning a pit dug up in the forest during the diviner's original initiation ceremony, is etymologically related to *kalunga*, or the underworld. After the diviner "steals" the basket, the basket maker curses him and wishes him death while she hits the "red ground" with a *mukenge* stick.

Sangombe too cursed humanity in all directions, wishing death and other calamities aloud so that Sakutemba would have many clients and be wealthy. Following the ceremony, Sakutemba would similarly attract new clients to himself by launching "verbal missiles" (Malinowski's expression) at humanity, while marking the ground with his *somo* horn. He would not wish people to die in the Angolan civil wars, shot by a rifle or blown up by a landmine, because such deaths are what they are and do not call for divination. People were bound to continue dying from the old but equally effective witchcraft attacks and continue suffering from all types of debilitating conditions, from illness to impotence. These were the victims of his verbal missiles, his potential clients.

But the diviners are witch-like themselves, and they will daub their eyelids with red clay. They take pride in describing themselves as *nganga*, meaning a well-established ritual expert with mighty powers, and as *valoji* (wizards and sorcerers). In a famous *lipele* song, they are described as eagle owls (*chikun-gulu* or *Bubo africanus* [Horton 1953:440]), a nocturnal species:

Lyaya lyaya	*Lyaya lyaya*
Kumbi mukalunga	The sun has set
Chikungulu kaliveye	The eagle owl does not miss its prey
Kushinganyeka kumbunge	And thinking is in the heart
Lyaya lyaya	*Lyaya lyaya*
Kumbi mukalunga	The sun has set
Vyalya mukweze vyavivulu	A youth eats much[15]

And yet diviners are vulnerable and at times compassionate. They fear witches in general and witches in particular—witches in the abstract, timeless sense that witches are always near and historical witches. People complained that the Angolan wars had forced many witches and wizards across the border. Then there were those witch-like or witch-for-real individuals who, out of spite, might report the Angolan refugees to the Zambian authorities. Old-time evildoers and present-time *delatores* share the evil feelings that spark their actions, often envy and rancor, and their duplicity, since they both appear to be cordial and amiable. From the viewpoint of emotions, they both incite fear. In an essay dealing with Uduk refugees in Tanzania, Wendy James describes the "structure of feeling" in which they lived at the time of her fieldwork: "You are worried, maybe about the state of your lost children . . . or about the presence of shades. . . . You may tremble, shiver, and lie awake in the dark" (1997:123). The Angolans in Chavuma lived in a similar "structure of feeling"—always alert and suspicious at the prospect of being caught, if not in one way, then in the other.

This explains at least partially the place of compassion in divination. Sangombe may have painted a picture of himself as a merciless, opportunistic farmer who in times of famine made high profits from feeding the hungry, but he also admitted that he would lower the price for his clients or return part of their money so that they could take the sick to a doctor. Once I asked him why he felt compassion for people whom he did not know personally or socially; was he not just doing his work, anyway? First he agreed with me just to be polite; then he explained that he and they were both sufferers, caught up in the same ruthless world, trying their best.

Basket divination, however, is not about the feeling and practice of compassion. Basket divination is about ritual efficacy, ontological shifts, truthful knowledge, and coping, four things that intrinsically are neither good nor bad. Its predominantly red symbolism is only befitting, for red is the color of ambivalence and moral indetermination (Jacobson-Widding 1979:358, 372). This very ambivalence invests the red elements with the power to destroy and inflict suffering, causing a sick man to perish to Kayongo, a diviner to be killed by a witch, a refugee to lose his or her personhood, or a subject to become an object. But ambivalence also invests the red color with a creative capacity, as when an ordinary man becomes a diviner, a basket a *lipele*, an ill individual a healthy one, a refugee a person, or an object a subject. Red operates in conjunction with, not only in opposition to, white. Red is imbued with "vital power" (Jackson 1998:86-87). Although we may speak of positive transformation in both cases, only in the latter does positive mean good. Transformation is always ambivalent and its results unpredictable. Order, solidarity, and good fortune are implicated with disorder, egoism, and misfortune. For the Luvale and others who were living in the shattered region of the Upper Zambezi prior to the end of the Angolan wars in 2002, that was being human. Life was red and white, and oftentimes more red than white; but as long as black—the color of social oblivion and nonexistence—was kept at bay, hope lived on.

3

Adulthood

When a newborn *lipele* is ritually initiated into divination, it becomes an oracle. An adult *lipele* is a personified basket, a basket endowed with agency, cognitive skills, and psychological traits. From the perspective of the diviner whose basket becomes an oracle, however, the *lipele* is much more than an awe-inspiring person who stands at the core of sociocultural life in south Central Africa. Basket divination is part of who the diviner is. It would not be far fetched to describe the *lipele* as a prolongation of his body, as Marx does the working tool.

Because the product of divination is ancestral knowledge, for which diviners charge high prices, the stage of adulthood brings us back to the role of commoditization in basket divination through the back door. After all, commoditization does play an important role in basket divination. The commodity, however, is not the *lipele* itself but the product of its labor—ancestral knowledge.

I never saw Sakutemba's new *lipele* at work. In line with my core methodology, I had intended to follow the cultural biography of Sakutemba's *lipele* into the stage of adulthood, but timing and communication difficulties got in our way, and, before long, my fieldwork had come to an end. I do know, however, that Sakutemba's *lipele* attracted many clients from near and far. In 1999, when I visited him again, he projected a new aura of success. I noticed that he had cared to purchase an expensive carrying basket for his *lipele*, and I was given the opportunity to meet several of his relatives who had meanwhile settled in his village. Now noticeably less concerned with disclosing his Angolan origins, Sakutemba described his neighbors as relatives from Angola who had barely escaped with their lives the latest upsurge of violence in the border region. The Angolan government troops were now pushing the

UNITA forces eastward, determined to win the civil war in combat since the failure of the 1994 Lusaka Peace Accord.

Missing the stage of adulthood in the cultural biography of Sakutemba's *lipele*, however, was not without consequences: if not Sakutemba and his *lipele*, then what diviner and adult *lipele* could I feature in this chapter?

In retrospect, I came to realize that my fieldwork mischance turned out to be a boon in disguise. Because the biographical approach to material things had led me to focus on the oracles and their respective owners, who would summon me on occasion to attend séances, I rarely knew the consulters and was ignorant of their predicaments, a lacuna that complicated my understanding of the divinatory speech. My fieldwork mischance enabled me to consider the clients' perspective. Basket divination, as Knut Graw puts it, has a defining "consultational quality" (2009:100). During the biographical stages of birth and initiation, previously described, the diviners and their baskets are the main focus of attention and the main goal of ritual action; during the stage of adulthood, however, they recede from awareness and become the means to an end—the revelation of knowledge. For this reason, and because, as mentioned, I never saw Sakutemba's *lipele* at work, this chapter deals with an adult *lipele* that belongs to a diviner chosen by his client, a young Luvale man named Chinyama.

The divination session I attended offered a unique opportunity: I knew well the consulters' party and the details of their predicament, which facilitated my comprehension of the divinatory speech; and I knew Mutondo, the selected diviner, whose older brother, village headman and professional senior (*mukulwane*) was no one less than diviner Sanjamba. I also hoped that by participating in the séance as a member of the consulters' party I would be able to overcome the reluctance on the part of diviners, men sharply aware of their profession's value for both insiders and outsiders, to allow unrestricted recording of their work. This reluctance, compounded by their fear to talk because of their political vulnerability as refugees, proved to be the major obstacle of my fieldwork.

Antecedents

In the dry season of 1996, Chinyama's son, Chuki, fell ill in Chitokoloki. Chuki's maternal relatives had consulted two different doctors (one from the mission hospital, and the other a traditional doctor who had diagnosed children's epilepsy),[1] both of whom had failed to cure Chuki. Then, in a moment of weakness, Chinyama committed adultery with his mother-in-law's younger sister, leading his in-laws to take his wife and son from him in a rage, deaf to his apologies and declarations of marital and fatherly love. Because he misbehaved and because he lived in a matrilineal society where children belong to their mother's kinship group, he could not stop them. But he did openly question their decision to move back to Luambo in Angola. What if the conflicts escalated? Having been born and raised in Zambia not far from the border, he knew well that Angolans continued to move back and forth across the international border, as they had always done (Hansen 1976:25-26). Yet he feared for his son.

When I first met Chinyama, he had just returned from Luambo. He was resting on a mat inside the mud-brick house of my friend Sapasa, his maternal uncle, who informed me that Chinyama had crossed the border under the cover of darkness and reached Chavuma before the first cockcrow.

Chinyama had brought bad news from Angola. If life in Chavuma was difficult, life in Luambo was appalling. There was plenty of land to cultivate and game to hunt in the forests and fish to catch in the rivers, but the most basic of material necessities were wanting. How can those people live without soap, cloth, and matches? he asked with a scornful tone that betrayed his Zambian upbringing. Were it not for the traders who carried processed goods from Zambia to trade for Angolan fish and game meat—here he teasingly pointed his chin at two large sacks of dried fish that he had carried on his bicycle from Luambo—the locals would bathe with water and revert to wearing bark cloth. In the same joking tone, Sapasa noted that the villagers in Angola and the villagers in Zambia were lucky to have each other, and even though the topic of conversation was very serious and perturbing, they laughed the laughter of sufferers who turn tragedy into comedy.

Then the conversation switched back to Chuki. Chinyama's mood suddenly darkened as he told us that his son's condition had not improved. Chuki's maternal relatives had taken action and consulted three different oracles: an axe handle (*mwishi*), a tortoise shell (*kapeza*), and a bottle (*mutumwa*). To Chinyama's alarm, however, these oracles had all blamed his own maternal kin who resided in Chitokoloki, south of Chavuma, where they had resettled in the 1940s to escape taxation and forced labor in colonial Angola. Depending on the oracle, Chinyama's relatives were accused of either bewitching Chuki or ensorcelling him with a Katotola mask (*likishi wakupanda*) that supposedly had appeared to the child in his sleep.

This news had greatly upset Chinyama. He had no recollection of his son mentioning such dreams, but he vividly remembered the day when both his son and ex-wife had dreamt of a hunter, a dream that the Luvale interpret as the manifestation of a displeased matrilineal ancestor. Could it be that the cause of Chuki's illness lay in the family of Chuki's mother? He had not shared this thought with his in-laws, but he had decided to take the matter into his own hands. On his way back to Chitokoloki, he would stop in Chavuma and invite his maternal uncle, a mature and wise man, to join him for a *lipele* consultation.

Sapasa's first reaction to his nephew's invitation was to express his deep concern and disagreement with the idea of consulting a *lipele*, the most powerful of all oracles, in the absence of Chuki's maternal kin. True though it was that social rules and expectations were changing rapidly, matrilineages still existed and had a say. Had Chinyama considered that the oracle might accuse his in-laws of witchcraft? How would he deliver such news to them (*kwaula*)? Witchcraft is always bad news. Chinyama's in-laws, if they were to be blamed, would rather hear that an ancestor of theirs had afflicted the child; after all, if Chuki had in reality been bewitched by his father's maternal relatives, as some of the oracles previously consulted had said, any treatment for the alleged ancestor-related disease would fail, and Chuki would die—in which case, Chinyama would be held responsible and fined heavily. In the light of Luvale customs and etiquette, Chinyama should let his in-laws handle the problem—their problem. But as is common in avuncular relationships in a matrilineal society, Sapasa cared for his sister's son and felt his suffering as if it were his own. Although his feelings and decision to help reflected the continuing importance of a relationship that is key in matrilineal societies, he justified his nephew's initiative with the fact that customs were changing rapidly anyway, the old figure of the maternal uncle (*natu*) yielding to the figure of the father (*tata*).[2]

Regarding the choice of diviner Mutondo, Sapasa agreed. Mutondo and his brother Sanjamba lived too far north from Chitokoloki to be cognizant of Chuki's predicament, which ensured the objectivity of the oracular pronouncements, but close enough to Sapasa, a partial quadriplegic. Furthermore, Sanjamba and Sapasa's fathers were distantly related and had both lived in the colonial township of Lumbala-Kakenge in Angola, where the Portuguese forces had relocated their families during the liberation war. In Sapasa's opinion, all these facts promised a pleasant stay at Sanjamba's village in Chilyakawa.

Sapasa also taught Chinyama what he should expect at the séance. He explained that a séance is like a conversation among the diviner, the consulters, and the *lipele*. Even though it has no mouth or ears, the *lipele* fully

18. Diviner Mutondo (Chavuma, 2002; photo by author)

participates in this conversation, and the diviner will address it as he would a person and will explain its answers—that is, the configurations of tossed symbolic articles—to his clients. He and Chinyama should listen to diviner Mutondo, respond, and ask back. Basket divination, he said, is about "asking one another" and "reaching an understanding." As a test to the diviner's professional authenticity, they should not smile, chuckle, grunt, hum, or give out nonverbal signs in reaction to his words because the origin of the divinatory knowledge should not lie in human interaction. The diviner, he said, is a mere "megaphone." He is not a fully intentional subject, his messages being imputed to a higher persona, Kayongo.

Note that Kayongo does here as he does during *lipele* initiation rituals: He possesses both the diviner and his basket, turning the diviner into an object and the *lipele* into a person. In both cases, Kayongo collapses ontological boundaries so that the diviner whose basket is being filled and the consulter whose predicament is under focus—diviner and consulter being here understood as simultaneously individual and collective entities—may reach de-objectification beyond ritual. *Lipele* initiations and divination séances, both costly endeavors, are always conducted for someone in need. Ontology is linked to existential imperatives; ritual is linked to everyday life.

Conversely, the resolution of existential imperatives, fleeting or lasting, calls for the activation of ontological shifts within the bounded space of ritual. De-objectification is not attained in a flash. As with the *lipele* personification, the revelation of ancestral knowledge requires the performance of a complex ritual in which the attendees must participate and show competence.[3]

In addition to focusing on the *jipelo* configurations, the consulters must know, for example, how and when to respond to the diviner's questions and interjections, how and when to ask back, which of the diviner's utterances call for immediate repetition, and when to clap in response to the diviner's snaps. Divining requires familiarity with many spoken and unspoken cues that refer to the content of divination as well as to the divinatory procedure (Goffman 1981:4). This is the reason Chinyama asked his uncle to join him at the séance. He was a "believer" (a Christian) who had never consulted a *lipele*. On his own, he would be lost, doubting at every step when to take the floor or give it back to the diviner and the *lipele*.

It turned out, however, that not even Sapasa's presence and words of advice fully prepared Chinyama. Alternately feeling acceptance, impatience, and exasperation, the diviner would hint several times at Chinyama's inability to ask back the right questions at the right moment. Consonant with the metaphorical understanding of divination as a journey, Mutondo would comment at one point: *Hatwama kulimbalaka* (literally, there is stumbling).

Writing Divination

Rebukes such as "there is stumbling" undo the spell of basket divination as performance. The process of revealing knowledge is intrinsically performative in the sense that it engenders the disclosure of knowledge. The spell of such content-loaded performances is to entice the participants to focus their attention on that content while letting form escape from awareness. Rebukes such as "there is stumbling" are especially valuable and illuminating because they bring formal structure and its metaphorical analogues to the fore.

How, then, to write a descriptive account that foregrounds content without letting form slip from awareness? Writing is a performative exercise as complex as divination and as liable to third-party scrutiny, and my solution is to offer as faithful and literal an account of the consultation as possible. Writing and editorial constraints imposed deep cuts on the original divinatory script. I am aware that my free translation of the abridged version that I present later in this chapter elides the zigzagging and repetition found in the original. I hope, however, to have preserved the overall structure, pace, and effect of the consultation.

In an attempt to describe things as they happened, I also describe the performative context in which people and material objects interacted and highlight the most important kinetic occurrences—the snapping, clapping, picking-up/shaking/putting-down the basket, and so on. To underscore the physical and spiritual basis of the diviner's speech (the fact that this speech is a transmutation of spiritually determined *jipelo* configurations into words), I both include photographs of the articles directly related to Chinyama's consultation and capitalize their names on their first occurrence. Other, less obvious references to these articles, as when the diviner refers to an article by means of synecdoches (for example, hunter, huntsmanship, bush, and game in lieu of GUN), remain lowercased.

Equally important in securing performative efficacy in basket divination is the role of metaphor. Metaphors "are means of doing things and not merely ways of saying things" (Jackson 1989:149; see also Lakoff and Johnson 1980:6). Divination is framed and experienced as a journey toward clarity. Note that the primary metaphors that define this experience—walking down a path and moving from darkness to clarity—are used in ordinary conversation, though not self-consciously. It takes skill to use these metaphors for ritual purposes while pretending, so to speak, that they are still quiescent. Analogously, because the path and clarity metaphors are as common and evocative in the English language as they are in Luvale—English speakers also return to previous points in order to make them clear—I attempt to reproduce both the elusiveness and creativity of the metaphorical speech by simply translating the Luvale into English.

Mutondo Divines for Chinyama

26 November 1996

Sapasa and Chinyama kindly agreed to let me attend and record their consultation. Chinyama had cycled to Chilyakawa at dawn to schedule our arrival, so around 11:00 A.M. we set off. We had a good time on the gravel road. Clad in a shiny, long-sleeve tracksuit in the heat of late November, Sapasa's teenage son, Chisola, insisted on pushing his father's wheelchair backward, making us all laugh amid the dust and racket.

On arrival in Chilyakawa we found diviner Mutondo awaiting us in his sling reclining chair. Chisola parked the wheelchair in front of Mutondo. We sat on small stools in a semicircle, enjoying the tree shade and a light breeze. After a brief exchange of greetings and small talk, Sapasa brought up my interest in videotaping and tape-recording the séance. Mutondo commented that a young white man (Boris Wastiau, a Belgian anthropologist) had recently visited him for the same reason, and added a pointed note about our wealth and their poverty, but he ended by acquiescing to the recording. Relieved, I shook his hand in gratitude.

No sooner had we sat down than Sanjamba appeared from behind a house, an ax on his right shoulder. He came to greet us, politely, but I sensed aloofness in his demeanor. I asked myself whether I should have requested his consent to record the séance prior to our visit. After all, the village was his, the *lipele* was his, and the diviner about to shake it, Mutondo, was his younger brother and professional junior (*kanyike*).

Mutondo went inside Sanjamba's house to bring out a large *kumba* basket containing the *lipele*. On his return, as the small size of our consulting party suggested a minor predicament rather than a case of death, he began to set up his *lipele* paraphernalia in the village plaza. He sat on a goatskin facing east, one leg outstretched and the other bent sideways. He signaled Chisola to bring Sapasa. Chinyama and I followed and sat on a woven mat in a semi-circle in front of Mutondo. A slim young man who was Mutondo's apprentice sat on Mutondo's right.

While I positioned my tape recorder and video camera, Mutondo opened his *kumba* and took out the *lipele* and its accessories. He placed his old, tattered *lipele* on the goatskin and set up a thick bundle of broken arrows (*mikuta yamivwi yavivimbi*) on the sandy ground, an arm's length aside. These arrows are tokens of consultations into the cause of death, given to diviners by the relatives of the dead. The thicker the bundle, the more respected the diviner. Other tokens of death consultations are thin strips of cloth torn from clothing once worn by the deceased, which diviners tie around *somo* horns. Mutondo set up his *somo* horn beside the arrows. To this ensemble of artifacts his acolyte added a metallic mug containing a powerful solution in which images appear. Other diviners use glass flasks instead of mugs, but they all like to complement basket divination with questions presented to these arcane oracles, usually referred to as *mitumwa*, bottles. Sakutemba, the diviner from Kalwiji, liked to call his flask "thermometer."

Mutondo unfolded the *lipele*'s animal skins, revealing the divination articles. Using powdered ochre stored in a small pouch, he traced four red lines on the basket's inner surface right below the edge: two on the side closer to him, and two on the opposite side, closer to us. With a round, solid piece of kaolin he drew one white line between each pair of red lines. These short white and red lines help the diviner determine the meaning of the *jipelo* configurations. As already explained, white is associated with purity, amity, and health, being used to mark the innocents at the end of consultations. Red represents danger. On the occasion of death consultations, the diviner will rub red clay on his eyelids. It is said that he is able to expose the evildoers and mark them with red clay because he knows, and may sometimes use, the powers of darkness.

Invocation, Kukombela

Mutondo opened the séance. He began by invoking chiefs, diviners, and national political leaders as he shook a dumbbell-shaped rattle called *musambo*. The rattling sound of this instrument and the soft, rapid utterance of the formulaic recitation are said to actualize the subjects of invocation and bring out Kayongo.

Now, who did Mutondo invoke? First, he invoked Semi and Mumba, two women who came from the East, Semi smiling and Mumba weeping, a formulaic reference to the historical origin of the local ethnicities in the southwest corner of the Democratic Republic of the Congo. Second, traveling across the ethnic and political landscape of northwest Zambia, Mutondo invoked the living and deceased chiefs of the Luvale, Lunda, Mbunda, and Luchazi. He started with the Luvale senior chief Ndungu and the Lunda chief Shima. He continued clockwise with the Luvale chiefs residing on the west bank and, crossing the Zambezi river again, he came to the Lunda senior chief Shinde, the Lunda chiefs Kahoshi and Nyakulenga, the Mbunda chief Sikufele, and the Luchazi chief Kalunga. Third, Mutondo invoked national figures whose politics have affected the lives of east Angolans: Frederick Chiluba, then president of Zambia, their country of exile; Mobutu Sese Seko, the late president of Zaire (now the Democratic Republic of the Congo), where over 160,000 Angolans lived as refugees in 1996 (UNHCR 1996); Agostinho Neto, the emblematic founder of the MPLA and first president of independent Angola, and Jonas Savimbi, founder and leader of UNITA until his death in east Angola in February 2002. Finally, Mutondo invoked diviners, those who are alive and those who have been buried or, in Mutondo's idiomatic allusion to the position in which corpses were buried in the past, "those who have descended with their legs bent and their feet upturned" (*washikumuka lyehi mukavunga mukono mukalumuna kavipundo*). He started with a few renowned diviners who once practiced in Angola and continued clockwise with the diviners living in Zambia in the mid-1990s, including his brother and professional senior, Sanjamba. The majority of the latter were Angolans from Moxico province who in the late 1960s had escaped the virulence of the liberation war, as UNITA and MPLA guerrillas based in independent Zambia attacked the Portuguese from the east.

19. Mutondo doing the invocation as he shakes a *musambo* rattle (Chavuma, 1996; photo by author)

By invoking such political figures as Chiluba, Mobutu, Neto, and Savimbi, diviner Mutondo openly recognized that his life, as well as the lives of
his clients, was implicated in large-scale phenomena that surpassed the local-
ism of Chavuma and even Zambia and Angola. Soon enough, Neto forged
alliances with Cuba and the USSR, Savimbi turned to apartheid South Africa
and the United States, and Chiluba embraced the new world order heralded
by the World Bank and the International Monetary Fund. By mentioning the
names of diviners who lived and died in Angola, Mutondo established a line
of cultural and historical continuity between a present in Zambia and a past
in Angola. By intentionally omitting the nationality of all diviners, particu-
larly those who were living in Zambia in the 1990s, Mutondo spoke obliquely
of the fears they shared as refugees.

Here is Mutondo's invocation, or *kukombela*:

Listen to me. "At sunrise the sun squirrel comes out while the night-
ape remains in the tree hole" [*Kunachi kunachela lyehi ngele, katoto
mulinda pako*].[4] It is now time for the invocation, let us invoke those
who came from the east, Semi and Mumba, Semi came smiling,
Mumba came weeping.

Whom shall we start with? We'll start with the chiefs. Who among
them shall we invoke? We mention Ndungu on the Mwalya [mean-
ing a stream in Mize], and Shima on the Kasese [in Chitokoloki]. As
we follow elephant footprints, to whom shall we return? We mention
Chinyama on the Litapi and Kucheka on the Kashiji [Southern Kashiji],
Kashiji and Litapi being alike. Next we find Nguvu, Nyatanda, Nyambi-
ngila, Salikishi, Nyakutemba [all on the Kashiji], Likila Sefu Mukila
waNgombe [between Kashiji and Lukolwe], Sanjongo Wotokela, and
Lingoji lyaMbwembwele [both on the confluence of the Kashiji and
Zambezi rivers]. We cross the Zambezi River and continue on the east
bank: Shinde, son of Kakunda [in Mukandakunda], Kahoshi son of
Ngenda, and we cannot leave out Nyakulenga [in the Upper Makondu],
Sikufele [in Manyinga], and Kalunga [in the Upper Mumbeji].

To whom shall we pay our respects, *kutapula*? [*Kutapula* means to
greet a high status individual by rubbing soil on the chest and clapping the hands lightly while standing on the knees.] Chiluba. But not
only Chiluba. Also Mobuto, Neto, and Savimbi. Neto and Savimbi
will never stop fighting.

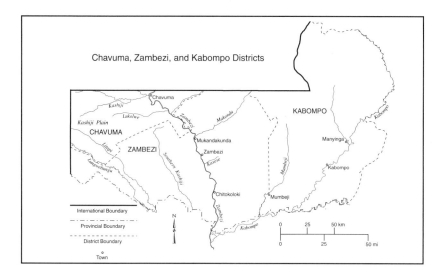

That's all, "Each xylophone key has a sounding-cup" [*Hapwa milingi kachi najinjimba*]. "As the sun rises, the dew dries away" [*Kucha chakumbi kuhunga chamume*].

Early this morning, while we were sitting here, a man [Chinyama] walked down that very path and said, "With water we bathe, with the *lipele* we discuss our problems." Then he left. In the late morning, how many persons walked down the same path? Four [Chinyama, Sapasa, Chisola, and I]. "We've come to stay," they said.

Tell us, *lipele*, what have they come for? Which portents do they want to disclose? "*Mipepe* and *mili*, human bodies and people" [*Hamipepe namili hamijimba hali vatu*, a proverb that stands for disease or ill human bodies, male or female];[5] they have come to learn about ill people.

To whom shall we now return? We'll return to the late great hunters [meaning the late diviners] who held this tool in their hands before passing it down to us.

Mutondo began with diviners Kavuma, Samakozo, Sandemba, and Kashinde, all of whom practiced and died in Angola. He continued with the diviners in Zambia, both those who were alive in the 1990s and those who had already "descended with their legs bent and their feet upturned," all the while following elephant footprints across the political and ecological landscape of east Angola and northwest Zambia. He ended with Kufumana chaPawa Mwiza Kukachim-bachila Ngimbu, Sanjamba's praise name. "I, Mutondo, talking today, am his slave," he said. As a preamble to closing the invocation, he brought the institution of basket divination to bear on the particulars of our séance: "'Each xylophone key has a sounding-cup.' 'As the sun rises, the dew dries away.' These ones sitting here, what have they come for? *Lipele*, explain what has brought them here. Tell us if they are deceptive, and tell us if they are truthful. Here we end. What will we do today? What has brought them here? We'll question one another."

Mutondo put down the *musambo* rattle, signaling the end of the invocation. A passerby greeted him by bending the knees and clapping the hands in a sign of respect, and Mutondo, momentarily stepping out of the ritual frame, greeted him hastily. Then he turned to us. He blew a speck of saliva into his cupped hands, clapped once, and shook hands with us all. *Ngungu-e, eh, putu, wala*, he said.

Like the act of laying down the rattle, the expression *Ngungu-e, eh, putu, wala* closed the invocation. Many recognize its formal role in divination even though they do not know its propositional meaning, suggesting that semantic obscurity has no bearing on formal effect (Bloch 1974:74, Tambiah 1979:163). Neither does semantic obscurity affect the ontological groundings of truth; as Niels Bohr, the Danish physicist, reminds us, truth is utterly unclear.

Divination Proper, Kutaha

After closing the invocation, Mutondo began to divine, *kutaha*. *Kutaha* is very loosely divided into three unnamed sections: The first section, which ends with the diviner putting down the *lipele* and saying *ngungu-e*, establishes a transition between the invocation and divining proper. By means of unsettling questions the answers of which are a priori known, the diviner lures his clients into seeing the baffling in the trivial and replicates discursively his clients' state of confusion by depicting conflicting scenarios. He also asserts core truths: ancestors can be invoked and put to good use, but they cannot resuscitate; the *lipele* is the most potent of all oracles; human suffering is caused by the hidden motives of the beloved; "that's all" (*mweka mwakwihi*). The second section corresponds to the revelation of the clients' predicaments and their hidden causes. The third section corresponds to the prescription of treatment or, in cases of death, to the allocation of guilt.

Divination proper has its own performative style. In sharp contrast to the invocation—a monologue uttered softly and in presto as the diviner shakes a *musambo* rattle—divination proper requires that the diviner, his *lipele*, and the consulters engage in a complex dialogue and bodily interaction. Addressing the *lipele*, the diviner poses a question—or utters an inquisitive, a conjectural, a confirmatory, or an excluding remark—by means of andante prose lines uttered in a neutral tone and moderate tempo. He shakes the *lipele*. The *lipele* answers back in the form of symbolic *jipelo* configurations. Pointing at key articles while gently swaying his torso, the diviner explains what he saw to his clients by means of short, rhythmic lines, uttered in a slightly raised pitch and quick tempo. These allegretto passages consist mostly of the answers given to the previous andante questions, and all the participants, including the diviner and his apprentice, will repeat them at once and in the exact same pace and intonation. (I omit these repetitions in the transcription below.)

Each time the diviner reaches a conclusion, he "gives" the floor to his clients by putting the *lipele* down and saying, "*Ngungu-e!*" The clients immediately reply, "Eh!" The diviner snaps his fingers, and everyone claps once. Only now do the clients confirm or deny his claims in a plain, colloquial style. They pose new questions to the *lipele*, a procedure called *kusukula*, and the session continues.

Now and then, in the long-phrased, andante style, the diviner sums up the new discoveries and may even reconsider his previous points in a new light or ask the *lipele* to confirm their veracity. Diviners move back and forth between monologue and dialogue, and formulaicity and colloquialism (Bauman and Briggs 1990, Wilce 2001). That they manage to do all this while sustaining a definition of the event is a remarkable accomplishment. To use a Luvale expression, the diviners have a *koze yayinene*, a great skill perfected over the years.

Diviners also step into and out of the divinatory frame. They reflect over previous conclusions in the process of divining, as mentioned; they greet acquaintances passing by; they walk away from the divination circle without warning, leaving their clients in suspense. But these are not the only possible moments of reflexivity during a consultation. In Chilyakawa, my recording equipment and I both fully participated in the séance and produced an alienating effect. The same was true for those standing nearby, including Sanjamba, who at one point took it upon himself to loudly denounce what he saw as the political and economic underpinnings of my fieldwork. He thus simultaneously participated and observed, much like I, the ethnographer, was doing.

In moderate tempo and neutral tone, occasionally waving his right hand to the rhythm of his own words, Mutondo proceeded to open the second section of divination, *kutaha,* by juxtaposing disquieting scenarios and leading his clients to see the baffling in the familiar:

Today, all the celebrated chiefs who stopped breathing and entered the ground will return to us, playing double-ended drums [a chiefly symbol]. Put everything aside, let's go and welcome the chiefs whose legs are bent and feet upturned.

Mutondo continued in quick tempo and slightly raised pitch, each short line being repeated once by all the participants in the exact same tempo and intonation:

Is this the way?
That's what we'll see
On this very day.

Shake! [Mutondo shook the basket and looked inquisitively at the *jipelo*.] As the articles denied his query, he concluded:

Ah, that's not the case.
The chiefs are gone.
We are all alive.
Only God gives death.
That's all.

Shake!

We must dig up *tuzeze* crickets [edible crickets that live in long, labyrinthine holes in the ground]; we must dig up *tuzeze* crickets. We must go back to where our friends [Sapasa and Chinyama] come from if we are to find what we are looking for. Will we fail in our endeavor?

Is this the way?

Shake!
Looking into the "bottle" and holding the *lipele* with both hands, Mutondo presented further unsettling scenarios:

I see many things lying in the village: a blanket, a dressing cloth, a coin, a pot, a glass, a calabash. They returned from the fields and found these things outside, flung all over the ground. No signs of robbery. A mystery.

Is this the way?
Have they said so?

Shake!

Ah, that's not the case.

So, I ask, were the cloth and blanket drenched in blood? Have they fallen from the clothesline? Why blood if no animal was killed? What happened?

Is this the way?

Shake!

Have these mysteries happened?
Ah, that's not the case.
Ah, listen well.
That's all.

Now Mutondo turned to Chinyama's predicament, suggesting that there is sickness caused by people.
Shake!

Ah, the "bottle" says,
We'll descend to
"The *mipepe* trees [men]
And the *mili* trees [women],
And the people
And their bodies."
If there is sickness
We will pick it up.
If there is deception
The *lipele* will tell.
These are my words.
This is the news.
I put down the *lipele*.
The oracle says,
With people only
Things began.

Ngungu-e!

All: Eh!

Snap! [Mutondo snapped his fingers, and everyone clapped once:]
Clap!

Sapasa: You're right, with people.

Having completed the introductory section of divination proper and
excluded the possibility of death, Mutondo moved on to determine the social
identity of the subject of divination, Chuki, now looking into the "bottle,"
now observing the *jipelo*.
    Shake!

With the very people. So I'll ask about them. We'll then proceed step
by step, posing each other questions. Are those persons grown-up
and married, or are they still with their mothers?

Is this the way?
What people?
Ah, married women?
Married men?
The oracle will tell.
Ah, that's not the case.
Listen well.
Straight to the children [CHILD, or Kanyike].
These *jipelo* are coming out repeatedly [*vanakakachila*, clinging to
    each other].
So, I ask, a boy or a girl?
Is this the way?
Ah, straight to the women [girls].
Ah, back to the men [boys].
Ah, listen well.
It's not a man.
Straight to the mothers.

Shake!

20. Child, or Kanyike, a divination article carved in wood (Museu Nacional de Etnologia, Portugal; photo by António Rento)

21. Man, or Lunga, a wooden figurine (Sakutemba's *lipele*, Chavuma, 1996; photo by author)

Ah, the oracle refuses.
She [the *lipele*] says,
We'll go to the men [MAN, or Lunga].
Here we'll descend.
That's all.
I give it to you.

Snap!
Clap!

Sapasa: You're right, sir, a boy. Let's continue.

Mutondo glanced over his left shoulder. A local trader had just arrived at Sanjamba's house, carrying a white sack filled with children's clothing from Katanga in the Democratic Republic of the Congo. The trader laid the sack on the ground and Sanjamba searched vigorously through the clothes. Mutondo proceeded to divine the cause of Chuki's illness:

Shake!

Why are all those problems afflicting the boy, so small and defense-
less? Listen, *lipele*, am I wasting my time? These things I am struggling with, are they correct? To explain them well, I must be pitiless.

Shake!

Ah, the oracle says,
Right here
Some dreams
Have come.
Were there dreams?
We'll ask.
I will take a breath,
So I give it to you.
The dreams
And the wailing [WAILER, or Katwambimbi],
Have they happened?
Ngungu-e!

All: Eh!

Snap!
Clap!

Mutondo: Right or wrong?

Sapasa: Right, dreams and wailing.

Mutondo, asking on behalf of Chinyama, who remained silent: He
confirms in awe. Is the wailing for the sick boy who will die, or is the
wailing for his fathers or mothers?

Is this the way?
He [Chinyama] failed to ask.
To whom is it for?
Is the wailing
For the father?

22. Wailer, or Katwambimbi, a wooden figurine in the mourning posture (Sakutemba's *lipele*, Chavuma, 1999; photo by author)

23. Path, or Jila, a grooved piece of wood (Sakutemba's *lipele*, Chavuma, 1999; photo by author)

Shake!

That's not the case.
She disagrees.
Let's go to the mother's village.
What has come out?

Shake!

Look well.
The wailing has come.
PATH [Jila] has come.
PLACE [Chifuchi] has come.[6]
And graves [GRAVE, or Mbila] for burying the dead [DEAD PER-
     SON, or Mufu].
What happened?
Ngungu-e!

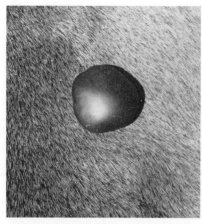

24. Place, or Chifuchi, a tree seed
(Sakutemba's *lipele*, Chavuma, 1999;
photo by author)

25. Grave, or Mbila, a calabash ring
(Museu Nacional de Etnologia, Portugal; photo by António Rento)

All: Eh!

Snap!

Clap!

Sapasa pressed Mutondo to identify the place where the funeral had been
held, Zambia or Angola, but Mutondo veered in a different direction:

Sapasa: What is that path and what is that place?

26. Dead Person, or Mufu, sometimes called Corpse, or Chivimbi, represented
by a corpse tied to a *mukambo* carrying pole (Museu Nacional de Etnologia, Portugal; photo by António Rento)

27. A corpse wrapped in cloth and tied to a *mukambo* pole prior to burial (Catoco area, Angola; in Schachtzabel 1923, illustration 10)

Mutondo: He asks how those things happened.

Shake!

Listen well.
I will explain
By means of these signs [*vinjikizo*].

Shake!
Mutondo observed the *jipelo* momentarily, then he pointed at a few:

Ah, a talking tongue.
A person tied up with a rope.
They called him SLAVE [Ndungo].
The WORD [Lizu] has come.

Someone had been accused of being a slave. After the consultation, Sapasa would explain that the accused person descended from a pawn, *topo*, an individual who had been given out by his relatives as payment for a wrong committed, never again being redeemed. The fact that pawnship

28. Slave, or Ndungo, a wooden figurine chained by the neck (Museu Nacional de Etnologia, Portugal; photo by António Rento)

29. Word, or Lizu, a small duiker horn (Sakutemba's *lipele*, Chavuma, 1999; photo by author)

is often represented in the *lipele* by a wooden figure displaying a chain or rope around the neck, material symbols of the Atlantic slave trade, suggests that slavery whatever its type is similarly experienced as captivity, being often conveyed by the same word, *undungo*. There is, however, an important difference between these types of slavery with regard to basket divination. Because pawns and slaves captured during feuds between villages were socially integrated into village life, their identity is still remembered, tainting social relationships among the living. Many such slaves were still common in Angola and Northern Rhodesia in the 1920s and 1930s (Cabrita 1954:71, White 1957:71). Slaves captured and taken away to the Atlantic coast beginning in the early nineteenth century soon lost social significance and fell into oblivion. Of these two categories of slavery, internal and external, only the former is represented in divination baskets.[7]

Staring at his clients:

I have no compassion,
I have no fear.

Speak up.
The oracle has paused.
Ngungu-e!

All: Eh!

Snap!
Clap!

Mutondo: Do you confirm?

Sapasa: Yes.

Mutondo, addressing Chinyama: Yes?

Sapasa, addressing Chinyama: Say something.

Shake!

Mutondo, once again reacting to Chinyama's silence and inability to ask back: Ah, so much stumbling.

Let me explain.
This word
Of slavery
Was heard.
I cannot hide.
It led to suffering.

Shake!

Mutondo: I'll pose the question myself; I ask, who is that slave? The one sitting here [Chinyama], or his wife and child?

Is this the way?
May the *lipele* be clear.
They meant you, the oracle says.
My friend,
They called you
Slave.

Shake!

That's not the case.
Listen well.
Let's enter your wife's village.
What has come out?

Shake!

Ah, concerns have.
And the one tied up with a rope.
You heard of chains.
You heard of slavery.
This is the explanation.
And I give it to you.

Snap!
Clap!

Mutondo: Right or wrong?

Sapasa: Where does the word of slavery come from? The family of his
in-laws or . . .

Shake!

Their FAMILY [Chikota, or matrilineal family].
Slave, they said.
I've run through
Their family problems.
Now I'll look
Into the things
Troubling the child.

Before he looked into the things troubling the child, however, Mutondo
revealed another important piece of information: An ancestor of Chuki who
had been a hunter in his lifetime and had accidentally shot himself in the
forest had been upset with his descendants because they had no *muyombo*

tree shrine where they could honor and invoke him and no *lukano* metallic bracelet representative of him on their wrist. This displeased ancestor had punished his female descendants with menstrual disorders and Chuki with a condition known as *ponde*, the same name used to designate all manner of violent accidental deaths, from drowning to snakebites.

Shake!

Ah, listen well.

The child has grandparents, mothers, older brothers and sisters. Do his mothers despise him? Will their witchcraft familiars kill him? Let me explain.

Is this the way?

Shake!

Ah, that's not the case.
Listen well.
The relatives
Of this woman
You have married
A-r-e s-t-r-u-g-g-l-i-n-g,

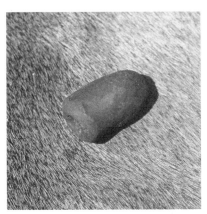

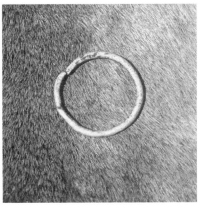

30. Family, or Chikota, a calabash stalk (Sakutemba's *lipele*, Chavuma, 1999; photo by author)

31. Lukano, a metallic bracelet (Sakutemba's *lipele*, Chavuma, 1999; photo by author)

Really struggling.
Between them
And their ancestors
I see many problems.

Shake!

Ah, let me explain.
Do they have *miyombo* tree shrines [LUKANO, a metallic bracelet
    symbolic of ancestorship]?
They have no *miyombo*.
The family has come.
In its middle
I can see
A hunter [GUN, or Uta].[8]
Listen to my words.
There is PONDE.
A sign
Of distress.

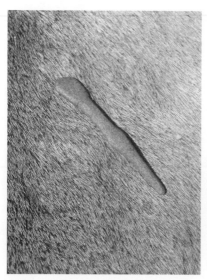

32. Gun, or Uta, carved in wood
(Sakutemba's *lipele*, Chavuma, 1999;
photo by author)

33. Ponde, a headless wooden figurine
(Sakutemba's *lipele*, Chavuma, 1999;
photo by author)

These are my words.
Ngungu-e!

All: Eh!

Snap!
Clap!
Mutondo glanced at Sanjamba, who now began to complain about my videotaping and tape-recording.

Mutondo, addressing Chinyama: As none of your in-laws is present, you yourself must speak up. Do you confirm what was said about your wife's family?

Chinyama: Yes.

Sapasa: Yes.

Mutondo proceeded to reconfirm his divination points:

Ah, listen well.

Are those things troubling the child linked to the *muyombo* tree, the *ponde*, and the hunter?

Is this the way?

Shake!

Ah, you've seen well
How things came together.
They walked down
This path.
This gun
Is the very hunter.
Here he died.
H-e-n-c-e t-h-e-i-r s-u-f-f-e-r-i-n-g.
He has caught the boy.
It is clear [*zwalala*].
He afflicted the child.

I will halt.
Anything you might have
To say,
Pack it in the *lipele*.
Ngungu-e!

All: Eh!

Snap!
Clap!
Now Mutondo turned to Chuki's symptoms. His right arm resting on the *kumba* and his gaze fixed on the "bottle," he said, "Now, what are the boy's symptoms?"
Shake!

Ah, listen well.
Let us answer
To their questions
About the nature
Of his illness.
"He who runs too fast
Ends up exposed in the plain" [*Kututa chikuma kulovoka kuchana*]
His legs
Are sore.
Ah, that's not the case.
His penis
Is swollen.

Shake!

Ah, that's not the case.
The oracle says
That to explain
This illness
We must enter
Inside the person.

Shake!

Ah, the boy had a fit.
Epilepsy.

Shake!

Ah, that's not the case.
The child will go mad.
His eyes
Are void.
Here the illness started,
And only then it spread.

Shake!

She refuses.
True or false?

Shake!

Ah, *she*'s agreeing after all.
The child is moaning.
Moaning in pain or moaning in madness?
Is this the way?
Crying.
He'll cry.
Ah, we stop at the sickness.
We've gone into the abdomen.
I will go no further.
From this potent source
Grew out branches
Into the whole body.
I stop here,
So we may cut down the fallen tree.
Ngungu-e!

All: Eh!

Snap!

Clap!

Mutondo: Right or wrong?

Sapasa: Right. Have your in-laws ever mentioned a hunter in their family? [He asked Chinyama.]

Chinyama: I don't know.

Mutondo, addressing Chinyama and showing signs of impatience: How can we unravel this point if you have come on your own?

Mutondo proceeded to summarize the main divination points disclosed up to then. He closed his speech by asking Chinyama the same question that Sapasa had asked him prior to the consultation: "How are you going to deliver the *lipele* news to your in-laws?" If the boy was to be cured Chinyama would have to involve his in-laws, but they would not be pleased to hear that their son-in-law had had the audacity to consult a *lipele* on his own account.
Snap!
Clap!

Sapasa, dismissive of the rights of matriliny: We want you to concentrate on what is making the boy so sick [*visako vyalyana*]. They can handle their own problems. We should put those problems aside, for we know nothing about them. Let them consult their own diviner.

Shake!
Mutondo refrained from further commentary on a thorny problem that did not concern him and moved on to the next step in his divination trajectory, the prescription of remedial measures. Pointing at the *jipelo*:
Shake!

Listen to me.
In the first place,
You must remove
The *ponde*.

Shake!

He'll trill and live happily.
There's something else.

After removing the *ponde*,

Shake!

Set up a small *muyombo*
And appease the ancestor.

At this point diviner Sanjamba summoned Mutondo, forcing him to interrupt his description of the cure and leave the ritual circle. We waited in silence. When, a few minutes later, Mutondo came back, he mechanically requested his payment, clearly following Sanjamba's instructions.
Shake!

Listen well.
At this point, my friends,
We must end.
It's now time
To receive my payment [*chikoli*].
Afterward
I'll describe the cure,
And you'll depart.
Ngungu-e!

All: Eh!

Snap!
Clap!

Mutondo, addressing Sanjamba: Sir, how much are they supposed to pay?
Sapasa: We had already agreed on the payment, 12,000 *kwachas*.

Mutondo, addressing Sanjamba: Sir! Would you collect this!

As Sanjamba ignored his request and continued to complain about my work, Mutondo collected the money. He counted the bills and handed them over to his apprentice. Sanjamba shouted that he knew very well what my intentions were: I had ordered a basket from basket maker Pezo, and his fellow diviner Sakutemba was teaching me divination; no doubt, I intended to make a fortune as a basket diviner in North America. "Isn't that so?" he asked the people who had meanwhile encircled us. "Yes!" they all replied. Sanjamba meant to say that I was just another foreigner who had traveled to their country to exploit them. Some white people wanted diamonds and animal skins; I was after their traditional knowledge (*chisemwa*). I wished to express my understanding, angst, and impotence, but, lacking the required fluency in the Luvale language and sensing that my view on the global political economy would be unwelcome at that moment, I commented instead, rather dully, that I too was a person (a Luvale tactic of soliciting empathy). Sanjamba switched the conversation back to *kwachas*. He demanded an additional sum of 8,000 *kwachas*, and threatened to charge Sapasa even more if my payment delayed.

Curatives and Further Knowledge

As soon as Sanjamba disappeared from view, Mutondo grabbed the *lipele*. His face looked as expressionless as before, but now he shook the timeworn basket so frequently and brusquely that some of the *jipelo* kept landing on the ground. Mutondo and his apprentice swiftly collected these *jipelo* between basket shakes. Mutondo proceeded to lay out in plain Luvale the curative procedures, reiterating that if Chuki's path were ever to "open up" (*te*) then the *ponde* had to be removed from his body and a small makeshift *muyombo* (*kamuyombo kakatengitengi*) set up by his relatives. Unlike with other, more costly *muyombo* ceremonies, here no animal or fowl would be slaughtered, no drums would be played or songs sung, and no *lukano* bracelets would be passed down from ancestors to descendants. All that was required would be a bit of white clay or cassava flour placed by the *muyombo*.

Something in the basket, however, led Mutondo back to the slavery accusation. We already knew that there had been a path leading to a place with wailing, and that an accusation of slavery had been voiced among Chuki's relatives. Now we would learn that the words of slavery came out at the funeral.

> Mutondo: Let me pose one more question. This boy is troubling me. As they fail to ask back, I ask about that path. Where was the child going?
>
> Is this the way?
>
> Shake!
>
> On the path

You are seeing
He walked.
That child,
Where is he?
We'll follow
This very Path.
Ngungu-e!

All: Eh!

Snap!
Clap!

Sapasa: Where did that path take the child?

Shake!
Mutondo, addressing Chinyama:

About the path.
Things happened.
Nothing on the father's side.
Listen well.
This path
Goes to your in-laws.
The *lipele* has spoken.
Ngungu-e!

All: Eh!

Snap!
Clap!

Sapasa: Why did they go on that journey? To visit their mothers?

Shake!
Mutondo continued:

There were greetings.
There was death.

Hence wailing.
Only greetings?
She will confirm.

Shake!

That's not the case.
One word uttered
Led to weeping.
That's all.
Ngungu-e!

All: Eh!

Snap!
Clap!

Mutondo: Right or wrong?

Sapasa: What words caused that illness?

Mutondo: Listen well.

Shake!

Ah, you've seen it well.
The funeral [OPEN FIRES, or Majiko].
This path brought problems.
The child went
With his mother
To a funeral.

Shake!

Let me explain.
Ah, listen well
To the explanation.
They talked
About people
At the funeral.

34. Open Fires, or Majiko, a wooden piece that represents funerals due to the open fires customarily lit at mourning camps (Museu Nacional de Etnologia, Portugal; photo by António Rento)

Shake!

And the word we mentioned
Was heard.
The word *slavery*.
Ngungu-e!

All: Eh!

Snap!
Clap!

Mutondo: Have you understood me? What do you have to say?

Sapasa: So, where did the funeral take place?

Mutondo: I've already explained. The oracle said that the funeral took place at the wife's village, not the husband's.

Sapasa, insisting: Where did it take place?

Shake!

Mutondo invited Sapasa to interpret the articles himself. At the third shake, Sapasa said, "Chitokoloki," supposedly confirming what he saw in the basket.

Mutondo: You've seen it well. What's this?

Sapasa: White clay.

Mutondo: Do you agree or not?

Sapasa: I agree. Was the relative who died in Chitokoloki a woman, a man, or a child?

Mutondo, assertively: I'm not divining that dead person.

Shake!

Yes. As the oracle explained, they went to a funeral. This path refers to their journey.

Shake!

An argument broke out and something was exposed [*kuvumbula*, to unearth], so that ancestor seized the child.

Sapasa: Where will the treatment take place? At the riverside, in dried land, or near a fallen tree?

Shake!

Now Mutondo proceeded to explain in a more colloquial tone the therapeutic procedures to be conducted by a doctor. This doctor should go to the end of a stream, poke a stick on the ground near a *musalya* tree [*Pseudolachnostylis deckendti* (White 1959:13)], and dig a small pit beside it. He should lower the boy into this pit and splash his body with medicine and brush it with a cockerel. The *ponde* would "clear out" (*zwalala*). Then, back in the village, Chuki's matrilineal relatives should plant a *muyombo* sapling and appease their ancestors. Enemas prepared by the doctor should be given to Chuki, as they would smell the *ponde* in the stomach and expel it. His path would open up (*pulungu*). At this point, in colloquial dialogue with Sapasa, Mutondo made his final divinatory point, correctly identifying Chuki's disease.

Sapasa: He really frightened the boy.

Mutondo: That hunter . . .

Sapasa: Yes, the sickness that came in that way.

Mutondo: The sickness lingered in the boy's stomach and then moved on to his chest and mouth. He started grumbling.

Shake!

He has taken medicines for children's epilepsy; am I right or wrong?

Sapasa: You're right, sir.

Mutondo ensured that Chuki would soon be "playing like a young calf." It was very clear (*hatoma to*). Then he said, "Let us receive white clay." Using the sharp tip of a wooden divination article, he scraped his kaolin stone and gave a few crumbs to Chinyama. He told us to take a pinch of powder from his right palm.

Sapasa: Is this white clay for rubbing on the body?

Mutondo: Right here above the heart.

Chinyama: Downward?

Mutondo: Downward, in the direction we exhale; inhaling stands for death.

Sapasa: We better do it downward!

Mutondo: Rub the white clay on yourselves, please.

Chinyama: Yes, sir.

Mutondo: The consulter who leaves without white clay above the heart is a witch or a sorcerer [*muloji*].

Mutondo asked me to listen to the recording. As I rewound the tape, Chinyama wrapped the white clay in a piece of paper and tucked it inside the wheelchair's back pocket. We shook hands with Mutondo in farewell and

35. A *kumba*, or lidded basket, used for storing and carrying the *lipele* and its paraphernalia (Museu Antropológico da Universidade de Coimbra, Portugal, cat. no. 89.1.289; photo by Carlos Barata)

rushed back home. When I last glanced over my shoulder, Mutondo and his apprentice were collecting the *lipele*'s paraphernalia inside the large *kumba*, which would then be stored beside Sanjamba's bed. We trekked down the sandy paths in silence. The moment we hit the motor road, Sapasa let out a complaint: Sanjamba had shamelessly ignored their patrilateral kinship; he had treated us like dogs.

Aftermath

On 27 November 1996, pushing an old bicycle loaded with sacks of dried fish, Chinyama set off to Zambezi, a stretch of eighty-four kilometers. He had acquired the fish in Luambo in exchange for sea salt, *vitenge* cloths, and fishing nets, and now he wanted to sell it at the Zambezi market, where prices were higher than in Chavuma. Meanwhile, he had decided that he would move to Luambo and win back his wife and child. The complications of life in Angola seemed less unbearable than before. The money earned at the market would pay for the services of a doctor knowledgeable in both *ponde* and children's epilepsy.

Chinyama did move to Luambo in early 1997, having obtained from the Angolan authorities a *guia de retornado*, the term in Portuguese for "return pass." Upon arrival, however, finding his ex-wife newly wedded to a local man, he had been forced to control his emotions and alter his plans: He could no longer win back his wife, but he could his son. In fact, amid his in-laws' constant brawling, it had been relatively easy to convince them that *their* child fared better in *his* hands and that the curative procedures would be conducted in Chitokoloki.

Maybe earlier in the twentieth century few men would have dared to voice such a request of their in-laws, much less put it into practice. In the 1990s, however, after over half a century of acculturation to the concept of paterfamilias through missionary education and labor migration to the mines and cities of three different countries—Democratic Republic of the Congo, Zambia, and South Africa—fathers were often more vocal and assertive and would negotiate with, if not confront, the old figure of male authority, the avunculus. As Sapasa once said, the days of "the cock begets, but the chicks are the hen's" (*Kusema chandemba vana vachali*), a Luvale proverb, were numbered, because more and more the hens were begetting, but the chicks were the cock's. To corroborate his point, Sapasa reminded me that his children were living in his village and not with their maternal uncle, a reality that had long been common in northwest Zambia (Katawola 1965:61).

But the wheel of fortune would spin again. In mid-2002, the last time I traveled to Chavuma, Chuki, cured of his ailment, was living with his paternal uncle in Chitokoloki. His father had moved to Zambezi to work in the cattle business. His mother and her second husband were staying at the Meheba refugee settlement near Solwezi. In 1999, the Angolan army had launched fierce attacks on the long-held UNITA territories of eastern Moxico. For the second time in their lifetime, they had been forced to flee.

A Way of Knowing

For Chinyama and Sapasa, the consultation in Chilyakawa worked: Chuki's maternal relatives had already enlisted the services of a doctor who knew the cure for epilepsy, a disease that the Luvale identify with the naked eye even though its cause is said to be unknown, even to diviners. Mutondo's diagnosis explained why the therapy for epilepsy had failed: it identified the agent behind this failure (a matrilineal ancestor of Chuki's who had been a hunter in his lifetime and had accidentally killed himself in the bush, a death called *ponde*), confirming Chinyama's suspicion and assuaging his fears that his family was to blame; it revealed the grounds for that ancestor's punitive action (his descendants' mutual accusations of slavery during a funeral and their having no *miyombo* tree shrines); it revealed the ancestor's mode of manifestation (a disease called *ponde*, like the accident that killed Chuki's ancestor); and it prescribed curative measures (for the epilepsy medication to work, the *ponde* had to be removed from Chuki's body; a *muyombo* tree had to be planted in the village to appease the late hunter; and the boy had to be treated with enemas). The séance facilitated the consulters' understanding of Chuki's disease and their collective predicament, and it offered a convincing diagnosis and a healing plan. Here in this capacity to promote understanding and move the consulters from uncertainty to provisional certitude and inertia to purposeful activity, if only temporarily, lies the intrinsic validity of *lipele* divination.

But how exactly is the efficacy of basket divination engendered? From the perspective of diviners and consulters, divination works because Kayongo is the source of oracular knowledge. His presence coincides, I argue, with the personification of the *lipele* and the objectification of the diviner so that the clients may become de-objectified. As ontological boundaries dissipate, turning what is otherwise perceived as discrete ontological categories into conduits for Kayongo, transformation—ontological, social, existential, and psychological—becomes possible.

Ritual and daily life are ontologically and existentially connected. The continuum object-subject encompasses the ritual and the secular not because all things living and nonliving are commodities, if not de facto, then *in potentia*, but because humans suffer with a passion and will take extraordinary measures to achieve, or at least come closer to, de-objectification. What makes these measures extraordinary is not their raw material—personification and objectification—which is abundant and ubiquitous, but their intentional and purposeful manipulation by experts within ritual.

Although the consulters are not said to embody Kayongo, they remain for the duration of the séance and posterior treatment within Kayongo's force field. This inclusion is achieved by a process of mutual incorporation: After closing the invocation, which serves to activate Kayongo, the diviner brings the clients into Kayongo's force field by spitting saliva into his cupped hands and then shaking hands with them. Later they return to their homes marked on their chest with white kaolin, a substance taken from the "material infrastructure" of the *lipele* (MacGaffey 2000:88). In cases of death, the consulters give the diviner material tokens of their dead relative—namely, a broken arrow or a strip of cloth torn from a piece of the deceased's clothing—and leave the séance with either a white kaolin mark on the chest, absolving them from guilt, or a red ochre mark on the forehead, accusing them of witchcraft—a tragic reminder that de-objectification is not always achieved. An accusation of witchcraft creates a witch, a nonperson. The red mark is a sentence of objectification.

Irrespective of outcome, however, basket divination is a way of knowing, a means of gaining access to ancestral knowledge—"the real" in Koen Stroeken's interpretation of Sukuma divination (2004; see also DuBois 1992). One never knows what will be uncovered or who the culprit will be or what the consequences of doing or failing to do what one was told will be. But it is because ancestral knowledge is deemed real that diviners stay in business and basket divination as an institution persists.

Yet, the revelation of knowledge and the consequent process of de-objectification (or further objectification through accusation), does not befall the clients instantaneously and miraculously, as cure does to those who were touched by Christ. The revelation of knowledge requires ritual work.

Conversing, Seeing, Feeling

Before delving into the workings of ritual, it is important to lay bare a few key premises of basket divination. Among these is the basic idea that it is up to the diviner to interpret Kayongo's messages as they appear materialized in successive *jipelo* configurations and to translate these for his clients into words. Victor Turner captured this aspect of basket divination in his description of the divinatory articles as "analytical" symbols. Because he never attended a séance, he was led to exaggerate the contrast between divinatory symbolism (the material symbols used in basket divination) and ritual symbolism (the symbols used in curative and life-crisis rituals). He claimed that although the semantic structure of the former exhibits "brittle segmentation," the cognitive and orectic poles of each material symbol remaining apart, in ritual symbolism those poles "fuse and condense," making these symbols synthetical rather than analytical (1975/1961:231-32). His insight that there is much thinking, rationalizing, and analyzing in basket divination, however, has withstood the test of time.

This is important because clients are after propositional knowledge. Drawing on fieldwork conducted among the Lunda of the Upper Kwango in the Democratic Republic of the Congo, de Boeck and Devisch tell us that the Lunda consulters do not fully understand the speech of basket diviners, often

Chokwe or Lunda speaking in Chokwe in too cryptic, poetic, and metaphorical a style (1994:111). In Chavuma, however, notwithstanding the fog of cryp-
ticness, poetry, and metaphor, the consulters not only show a considerable
level of comprehension but also see divination as a conversation.

Supporting evidence is everywhere: "What will we do today? What has
brought them here? We'll question one another," Mutondo said as he closed
the invocation. Basket divination is about "asking one another" and "reaching
an understanding," Sapasa explained to his nephew prior to our departure to
Chilyakawa. It is not a coincidence that the divination basket was once known
as *chipoza*, a Chokwe word derived from an obsolete verb meaning "to converse" (Bastin 1959:101, Lima 1971:116). The contemporary word *katachikijilo*,
sometimes used when referring to a divinatory article, means a sign, a token,
a mark, a means of knowing something that can be spelled out; it derives
from the verb *kutachikiza*, meaning to know. The term *chinjikizo*, another
term for a divinatory article, derives from *kwinjikiza*, to know thoroughly.
Similarly, the word used to denote the diviner's erudition is *chinyingi*, which
derives from the verb *kunyingika*, meaning "to know," which the Luvale bor-
rowed from the Chokwe (Horton 1953:269).

In addition to being propositional, divinatory knowledge is visible.
Basket divination offers spiritually authenticated information by means
of material configurations. I am not saying that consulters have or claim
the ability to interpret the symbolic configurations as they land inside the
basket. Chinyama and Sapasa, for example, promptly admitted that diviners shake their baskets too often and rapidly, and they struggled to recall
the articles that emerged in Chilyakawa. Their sense of ritual efficacy did
not stem from their ability to decode *jipelo* symbolism but from the fact
that this symbolism, expressing itself in material configurations, enabled
the externalization, visualization, and manipulation of their predicament.[9]
As a "neutral object," Jackson would say (1989:149-50), the *lipele* enables
distancing and understanding. Other arcane oracles such as the "bottle,"
frequently used in Chavuma, also convey messages by means of images,
but these images are only discernible to the diviner. To those who lack
enhanced sight, the *lipele* has accrued merit because it communicates by
means of configurations that are visible to all.

This emphasis on sight pervades basket divination. The Luvale word
mukakutaha, like its English translation "diviner," is synonymous with "seer."
To divine is to see, and to see is to know. A *chitaho* (from *kutaha*) is both
synonymous with *ngombo*, meaning any material object used for divining,

and a particular type of oracle consisting of a container filled with medicated water, often a mortar, into which the diviner peers to see the knowledge. The diviner's eyes are said to be sharp like the eyes of an eagle-owl (*Bubo africanus*). He received his gift of clairvoyance during his initiation ceremony, when medicine was applied to his eyes to clear his vision and remove the blur characteristic of ordinary eyes.

Because social scientists are part of a long intellectual tradition whose epistemological vocabulary is one of seeing—the ancient Greek verb *noein*, for example, means both to "think" and "to see," and vision continues to stand in contemporary science and philosophy as the root metaphor for clarity (Edie 1963:551-52)—the interpretation of basket divination and other visualist divinatory techniques as Positivist science is tempting. But lest the analogy between divination and Positivist science be pushed too far, let us remember that the basket diviner is not a Cartesian seer, an observer of static and mute objects. He does not reduce vision to what Don Ihde (1979:chapter 7) and Johannes Fabian (1983:105-42) call an objectifying gaze, detached and above the things seen, or thought and the divinatory experience to vision. The delivery of propositional knowledge is a practical activity that enlists several sensory modes in addition to vision. The diviner must shake his basket with his hands, the principal instrument of the sense of touch, and Kayongo must possess him as well as his basket, causing pain in his chest. Only when he utters the right pronouncement does the pain subside. Needless to say, pain is a highly effective mode of communication, since, of all sensory modes, it is the only one that hurts, placing on the sufferer an "affective call" (Leder 1990:73; see also Stoller 1989b, 1997). To deliver scientific, Positivist knowledge is allegedly a painless, disembodied exercise; to deliver divinatory knowledge is painful.

The diviner's feelings of pain and relief are celebrated in a *lipele* song:

| *Kapalakanyi uno ngombo yami* | That feeling of pressure, my *lipele* |
| *Ngombo kahehula ngombwe* | This feeling of lightness, *lipeleee* |

The link between knowledge and the heart is not simply reflexive, the brain responding to a stimulus in the heart. For the Luvale and related peoples, the heart is also a site of thought. People say that they "think in the heart" (*kushinganyeka kumuchima*), and diviners wish that their hearts may have openings of understanding like the openings of a banana stalk. Sangombe explained: "Let the throat have openings [*miteta*], let the heart have openings. When the diviner lays his hands on the *lipele*, may he have openings of understanding [*miteta yakushinganyeka*] like the openings of a banana stalk. A man's heart has openings like a banana stalk. This is no trivial matter. When the heart in the chest hurts, kwi!, you start moving like the cowry shell moves in the river sand. This is how it is."

De-Objectification as Performance

Consulters expect propositional knowledge that has axiomatic validity. The source of knowledge is Kayongo, and Kayongo reveals the truth. I was told that diviners grasp the truth as soon as their clients arrive. Sapasa, for example, reminded me that Mutondo had mentioned Path and Words early in the séance, a fact that to his eyes constituted irrefutable proof that Mutondo had known the truth all along. Yet, prior to our departure to Chilyakawa, Sapasa explained to his nephew that to divine is to engage in a conversation and reach an understanding. The translation of truth into the medium of words requires the conduction of a ritual in which both diviners and consulters play a role. In the end, ontology and performance are both critical and truthful.

In the remainder of this section, I focus on the workings of ritual. My overall argument in this book has been that the personification of the *lipele* and the objectification of the diviner within the context of ritual are always linked to a process of existential de-objectification outside ritual, however fleeting. Here, I describe the way in which ritual action engenders this process of de-objectification. I see the diviner as a master of ceremonies whose role is to lead his clients to experience their search for knowledge in bodily and performative terms. I suggest that he does this by discursively defining the complex structure of the séance as a long, gradual journey toward clarity.

I begin by reminding you that every *lipele* consultation is composed of a fixed bipartite structure that invariably begins with the invocation and proceeds with divination proper. By far the longest and most elaborate, divination proper is subdivided into three parts: The first part seeks to assert core ontological principles, replicate the consulters' state of confusion, and sensitize the consulters to see the inscrutable dimensions of everyday life; the second and third parts bring Kayongo (and a host of diviners, chiefs, and heads-of-state, dead and alive) to bear directly on the specific case raised for divining. Performatively, however, all three parts are further subdivided in a variable number of similar units that consist of variations on a fixed sequence: The diviner poses a question, shakes the *lipele* a few times, observes the resulting *jipelo* configurations, translates them into words, hands over a statement, puts down the *lipele*, says *ngungu-e,* snaps, claps once with his clients, and they ask back (or the diviner will ask back himself lest the consultation come to a standstill). By escorting his consulters through this formal structure in which human bodies, artifacts, and words interact with one another, the diviner effectively propels the ritual forward and suggests a sense of progression.

In tune with the importance of verbalization and conversation in basket divination, however, it is at the level of speech that the diviner's skill is most complex and spectacular. *Lipele* diviners engender a passage from confusion to understanding by replicating and enacting this passage at the level of discourse. Richard Werbner and David Parkin reached a similar conclusion in their respective work among northern Tswapong wisdom diviners in Botswana and Giriama and Swahili diviners in Kenya, with Werbner phrasing that passage as a movement from "baffling complexity" to "intelligible complexity" (1989:59), and Parkin describing it as a movement from simultaneity to sequencing, "jumbled speech" to "sequential speech" (1991:185).

To enact this passage from darkness to clarity, *lipele* diviners begin by recreating discursively their clients' deep fears and muddled thoughts in the opening part of divination proper. Mutondo said at one point: "I see many things lying in the village: a blanket, a dressing cloth, a coin, a pot, a glass, a calabash. They returned from the fields and found these things outside, flung all over the ground. No signs of robbery. A mystery." Consulters fear evildoers, and the diviners will voice those fears through depictions of baffling scenarios. But the diviners do not dwell long on this initial divinatory stage and will shortly proceed to engendering the desired state of clarity by discursively teasing out a sequence of propositions. One strategy, which *lipele* diviners share with Tswapong wisdom diviners in Botswana, is to control the conversation with the oracle by phrasing key questions as variants of "if-then" propositions (Werbner 1989:46):

What people?
Ah, married women?
Married men?
The oracle will tell.
Ah, that's not the case.
Listen well.
Straight to the children.
These *jipelo* are coming out repeatedly.
So I ask, a boy or a girl?

The diviner asks if the object of divination is a married person. The *lipele* denies, so he considers the possibility that it may be a child—if not A, then B. Now, is it a boy or a girl—if B, then C or D? The revelation of truth is incremental, building on previous conclusions one step at a time. Now and then, between new inquisitive remarks, the diviner confirms and reconfirms previous divinatory points as he peers into the "bottle" and back to the *jipelo*.

Another discursive strategy is to carefully delineate the divinatory path and avoid sidetracks. At one point, Mutondo reminded Sapasa that the subject matter of his consultation was the boy's sickness and not the dead person whose funeral came up: "Was the relative who died in Chitokoloki a woman, a man, or a child?" Sapasa asked; "I'm not divining that dead person," Mutondo replied. Earlier in the session, Sapasa had resorted to the same tactic to orient the questioning in the direction that best suited his nephew's interests; in his words, "We want you to concentrate on what is making the boy so sick. . . . They [the boy's matrilineal relatives] can handle their own problems. . . . Let them consult their own diviner."

My description of divination in terms of the primary bodily experience of walking down a path is not fortuitous, for this is how the diviners discursively frame the revelation of knowledge for their clients. Mutondo spoke of crossing and re-crossing the Zambezi River as he followed the footprints of mighty elephants (meaning the senior chiefs and diviners), both those who lived in the woodlands on the eastern side and those who lived in the flood plains on the western side. He did not list personalities in a virtual table or place them on a map—Casey's indifferent "site-space of cartography or rational geometry"—but walked through "places" in a familiar social territory (1987:195).

If in invocation Mutondo followed elephant footprints (*kukoka matende*) across the Kalahari sands, in divination proper he followed *jipelo* configurations. His divinatory journey was a rich social experience and one in which people and objects engaged in conversation and bodily interaction. Together, Mutondo says, the séance participants "set off," "walked" down a path, "halted" at new discoveries, "entered" or "descended" into problems, "ran" through minor matters, and "returned" to previous points. On reaching a conclusion, Mutondo "put down" the basket, "took a breath," and "gave" the news to his clients. These, in turn, "packed" the basket with new questions, and the journey continued. At each step, Mutondo asked the *lipele, Mujila nyi omwo?* (Is this the way?) He wanted to ensure that the group would not follow the wrong path and go astray. And as happens with other travels, he hoped for a pleasant journey in which the participants walked together at the right pace, not so fast that they would end up in an open plain, exposing themselves to danger (as suggested in a proverb quoted by Mutondo), and not so slowly that they would stumble and fall. The divinatory journey, irrespective of the speech's velocity, ought to be poised, cold-headed, and incremental.

The divinatory journey begins with mystery, uncertainty, and passivity, and it progresses gradually toward revelation, certainty, and resoluteness. As the participants move along a journey with a direction and a goal, both a set of responsible agents and a ground for future action are revealed. To use another metaphor commonly used in the Upper Zambezi in the context of affliction rituals, darkness gives way to clarity.

This movement from obscurity to clarity, which as walking along a path is a primary bodily experience, is repeatedly evoked through the action of bringing something to the surface, as one does while "digging up *tuzeze* crickets." So one "descends" or "enters" the depths of the unknown to bring an answer into the open or, other times, one merely scratches the surface of a topic, choosing not to halt and descend into it. Another powerful way of evoking clarity is through the use of certain ideophones—*zwalala, to, pulungu*—as well as proverbial expressions in which clarity comes with the sunrise: "At sunrise the sun-squirrel comes out while the night-ape remains in the tree hole"; "As the sun rises, the dew dries away." In a similar vein, the diviner is described as a crowing rooster that announces the sunrise. Once the sun has risen, which is the same as saying, once the journey has ended, darkness has become clarity, and the oracle has uncovered the culprit, *ngombo yinamusolola.*

The diviner is a rooster in a different sense, too. One of the words denoting the divinatory act, *kusanda*, means to scatter or scratch out the earth like a fowl. The diviner shakes his basket like the rooster scatters the earth, suddenly and jerkily (Hauenstein 1961:124).

Now, why is the use of metaphor efficacious? Jackson says that "metaphor reveals unities . . . metaphor reveals, not the 'thisness of a that' but rather that 'this *is* that'" (1989:142; his emphasis). The revelation of divinatory knowledge may at times be abstract and cabalistic, but through metaphor it becomes a familiar experience. Divination becomes a journey from darkness to clarity. Speech, knowledge, and the body coalesce.

The Color of Clarity

Yet clarity, as a phenomenon, remains altogether unclear. What is clarity, really? Does it stand for health, amity, and solidarity, like the color white does? Is clarity white? Turner's famous description of basket diviners as judges and basket divination as a mechanism of social redress suggests that clarity is white, and white is the color of social order (1975/1961). De Boeck and Devisch argue that this interpretation speaks louder of the influence of structural functionalism on Turner's early work than of basket divination, and they note that consultations may worsen the crisis rather than resolve it (1994:110, de Boeck 1991:159-60). Chinyama, I remind you, took his son away from his relatives, who promised that they would set up a makeshift *muyombo* to appease their ancestors and to overcome their differences. Chinyama, however, had returned to Zambia in haste; he could only speak for what he had seen and heard in Angola—his in-laws' "constant brawling."

This said, I would argue with Turner that in northwest Zambia, and south Central Africa more generally, social order is clear white. Whiteness, however, is best described as a social ideal that more often than not is at odds with social practice. For the Ndembu whom Turner describes in his early work (1957, 1967, 1968, 1975), there is a direct link between social well-being and physical well-being. Such ills as disease, infertility, impotence, and death derive from severed or strained relationships, being ultimately healed or resolved through rituals in which grudges and ill feelings are voiced openly. Diviners reproduce this social and medical system by prescribing the conduction of such rituals; they do not claim that social order will be achieved and made real.

Turner himself recognizes that basket divination is full of red symbolism that flies in the face of social order. In "Muchona the Hornet, Interpreter of Religion," Turner says that Kayongo is a ritual "full of red symbolism standing for killing, punishment, witchcraft, and in general, for violent breach in the natural and social orders" (1967/1959:143). He goes so far as to feel that "there is an aspect of unconscious revenge against the social order in divination" and, in Muchona's case, to speculate that "beneath his jester's mask, and under his apparent timidity, he may have cherished hatred against those more securely placed in the ordered groupings of society" (1967/1959:146).

When Muchona the judge is divining, however, he is no longer Muchona the revengeful; now he is the supporter of collective morals and social values, he is caught up in his role and enthralled in performance. Turner correctly distinguishes between the self and the role, Muchona the individual and Muchona the "upholder of tribal morality," who also happens to be Muchona the vessel for Kayongo (1975/1961:242). In his words, "In concentrating on the special problems posed by his clients, the diviner ceases to be his everyday self, swayed by self-interest and ephemeral desires and ambitions. He is a man with a vocation. He measures actual behavior against ideals" (1974:230).

I do not mean to say that diviners do not recognize the redressive potential of basket divination. On occasion, they may even lower their charges, momentarily becoming philanthropists. In my experience, however, basket diviners do not see themselves as heroes bound to rid the world of dissent and disease. Maybe the world they knew was ill beyond cure. They had lived in a country torn by war. They had fled for their lives and resettled in an overcrowded and resource-depleted place where relatives turned against relatives and wars were waged through sorcery, witchcraft, and threats of denunciation to the Zambian authorities. Ill feelings were endemic and society seemed chronically ill. As diviners, all they did was perform their rituals, help their clients as best they could, and expect payment for their work.

Are diviners judges then? I would say that they are, from a scholarly perspective. Metaphors bring the familiar to illuminate the unfamiliar in ways that jolt and surprise. To describe diviners as judges, as Turner does, is to say that diviners, much like judges, work within the parameters of the law and its sociocultural and political enmeshments. As judges, they both operate with "the universally recognized concept of the 'good man' or 'moral man,' *muntu wamuwahi*" (Turner 1975/1961:238), and in neither case is their professionalism questioned when their sentences worsen the crisis rather than resolve it. In fact, both diviners and judges benefit from hate, dissent, and crime, their raw materials, of which there never seems to be a shortage. Medical doctors also deal with the less dignifying side of humanity, and it is no coincidence that young, structural functionalist Turner draws on this metaphor as well. The diviner, he says, "'feels after the stresses' and sore points in relationships" and sees his task as "remedying the ills of the corporate group" (1967:392). More intriguing perhaps is his portrayal of diviners as politicians. "Divination as a system of thought," he says in a footnote, "exhibits the 'paranoid style,' but diviners regard themselves as acting in the public interest—compare politics and politicians in Western society!" (1975/1961:242). Predating later interpretations of diviners as scientists (but, alas, scientists demoted to Positivists), Turner also portrays the basket diviner as a social analyst and a logician (but, alas, a logician demoted to a magician) (1975/1961:235, 241).

"Judge," "medical doctor," "Positivist scientist," "artist"—these are all equally thought-provoking metaphors—from a scholarly perspective. The problem with such metaphors, as Turner acknowledges, is that "even though they draw our attention to some important properties of social existence, they may and do block our perception of others" (1974:25). To ensure not only scientific insight but also ethnographic concordance, scholars would do well to take note of local metaphors. In 1990s Chavuma, the basket diviners I met spoke of themselves as workers. For an elitist spirit, maybe "worker" is less refined than "judge," "artist," "scientist," or even "doctor." At a time and place in which diviners struggled daily to survive and earn a living, however, "worker" spoke louder and felt closer to their experience.

Diviners were also aware that basket divination has always been a risky profession. Clarity as whiteness may be a laudable social ideal, but the individual who at the end of a séance is accused of witchcraft may disagree and take revenge. What the white-marked innocent will perceive as relief, the red-spotted culprit will perceive as punishment, if not downright injustice. What the innocent will perceive as clarity, the culprit will perceive as darkness. Clarity is not always clear. Those diviners who once fell to the wrath of the accused serve as a reminder of this basic truth.

Have you heard of Kandemba, the ill-fated diviner from Angola? Sangombe once asked me half humorously, half nervously. Kandemba had been summoned to a village in Angola, where he accused his own client of having bewitched the dead person. Humiliated and enraged, his client had speedily pulled a knife from his sheath and stabbed Kandemba to death. Kandemba's assistants reciprocated in kind by stabbing the murderer repeatedly, but Kandemba was no more. Hence, the song:

Kandemba, Kandemba	Kandemba, Kandemba,
Ngombo yamulya	The lipele killed him
Kandemba	Kandemba
Ngombo yamulya	The lipele killed him
Eh mame	Eh mame
Kechi kumona chendo chamapwevo	To the sight of women passing by
Meso mwalezula	His eyes rolled up [as in fainting].[10]

For this reason and because they speak Kayongo's truth, diviners always insist that they occupy a neutral ground: They do not voice their personal opinion; they talk what they are told to talk. Why then should they be responsible for what is said and done after divination? As Sangombe put it proverbially, "The one who made your fishing net is not responsible for your death in the river" (Ove unatungu lyoji, ami nangwiza nakulanda, ami nanguya nangukafwa ponde halwiji).

I would thus say that the color of clarity is utterly unclear. As a spiritually validated social ideal that is often at odds with sociological realities and individual experiences, clarity is white—which helps explain why young Turner, writing in the eddies of structural functionalism, a "white" theory, was drawn to whiteness. As divinatory knowledge that leads to accusations of witchcraft and social cleavage, clarity is scarlet red. Clarity then is both white and red, as argued in Chapter 2, a pair of colors not always peaceful but notoriously effectual and transformational.

In this chapter, which deals with the stage of adulthood in the life of a *lipele*, I have focused on the workings of ritual and less so on its consequences. Kayongo manifests himself as a personified object whose messages are translated into the medium of words by the diviner, a man turned into an object. It is said that Kayongo reveals the truth in a flash, but unless the diviner and his clients engage in a long, structured talk framed as a journey toward clarity, de-objectification is impossible. Had Victor Turner had the opportunity to attend a séance and record the divinatory speech, rather than relying mostly on private interviews with Muchona and an Angolan Ndembu diviner on a visit to Zambia (1975/1961:243-44), he would have probably realized that basket divination is a journey toward clarity. Divination is also revelation. Here the analytical and the synthetical are highly "fused and condensed," and divination is expressed in a revelatory mode.[11]

Inverting an old dichotomy in Western social thought between knowledge and belief (Quinton 1967) and between "our" knowledge and "their" belief, I would therefore conclude by saying that while Positivism rests on the belief that all things bodily, emotional, and existential are irrelevant and detrimental to true knowledge, basket divination presupposes the knowledge that divinatory statements cannot be achieved through intellectual reasoning and vision alone, but rather equally entail spiritual embodiment, physical pain, and practical skills. Reversing Horton's Popperian contrast between open and closed predicaments (1993/1967:153), while Positivism is closed in the sense of being exclusive, simplistic, and nonreflexive, basket divination is open in the sense of being inclusive, holistic, and reflexive. I would therefore refrain from comparing the diviner to a Positivist scientist in order to rescue him and Africa from the murkiness of belief, and I would instead highlight a different kind of truth—divinatory knowledge is at once a spiritual, intellectual, embodied, and performative accomplishment, and its truth or value ultimately lies in its capacity to release states of existential obstruction and restore relations with others, living and nonliving.

Conclusion

A Way of Living

The *lipele* is caught in a lifelong ontological ambiguity, being simultaneously subject and object, spirit and matter, person and tool. It is endowed with that quality that Pietz calls "irreducible materiality" (1985:7), and yet it is empowered.

This idea of irreducible materiality is at least as old as the Latin origin of the term "fetish," *facticius*, which means "made" or "manufactured" (Pietz 1987:24). Despite the weight of intellectualism in the history of social sciences and humanities, a number of scholars have given due credit and much thought to the materiality of such entities, now perceived as art. For anthropologist Robert Armstrong, African sculpture has "presence," a quality that belongs to the realm of feelings and affect rather than intellect (1971). For art historian Arnold Rubin, the way in which different materials are assembled and reconfigured in African sculpture is visually striking, and he attempts to capture this powerful effect with his descriptive concept of "accumulative sculpture" (1993:21).

Few scholars, however, have taken an interest in the old concept of fetish. Avant-garde artists had earlier resuscitated and refashioned this concept as art, with Minimalist sculptor Carl André stating, "Works of art are fetishes; that is, material objects of human production that we endow with extra-material powers" (quoted in Baker 1988:36). But it would take longer for scholars to distance themselves from the term's tainted origins in nineteenth-century intellectualism. Maybe scholars have sensed all along that the act of flipping the term around and removing all traces of negativity does not save it from what it has always been across the disciplines—a concept turned upon itself, a monad. "Fetish" always smacks, if not of downright delusion, then certainly of misdirection, excess, fixation. "Fetish" always smacks of "fetishism."

In this book, which deals with the place of ontological fluidity in human life, I have given priority to the historically contextualized understanding of the *lipele* not in itself but in relation. Drawing on the fieldwork I conducted in northwest Zambia in the 1990s, I have shown that the personification of divination baskets and the objectification of diviners within ritual, often discussed in the literature as *fetishism* and *possession*, respectively, are not only mutually entailed but also existentially and socially linked to the de-objectification of the diviners and their clients outside ritual. The sacred and profane may be spatially distinct, but they are not disconnected. For those seeking de-objectification, basket divination is a way of doing things through ritual, a way of knowing the truth, and a way of working and laboring.

We should not confuse fetishistic interpretations of fetishes, scholarly or artistic, with the experience of fetishes in Africa. These material entities have presence and potency most certainly, but they are not solipsistic. Their mode of being is intersubjective, and their significance, in addition to being religious, moral, symbolic, artistic, social, economic, and political, is also existential.

Ex-commodity

If not "fetish," then what? The term *ex-commodity*, meant by Appadurai as a thing that begins its career as a commodity—a thing exchangeable for other things or money—only to be quickly removed from the commodity state (1986), is further distanced from the lifeworld of its denotatum, the *lipele* itself. Unlike *fetish*, *ex-commodity* is relational (ultimately derived from an act of exchange) and politically innocuous (free of derogatory overtones); like *fetish*, however, *ex-commodity* is disconnected from the intersubjective and existential significance that the *lipele* has for its users.

I was originally drawn to commoditization theory. It resonated well with my determination to eschew the Positivist concern with what kind of thing the *lipele* is and provided me with both a method of data collection and a sizable terminological kit with which to conceptualize that data. Its broad spatial and temporal range also served as a reminder that divination baskets are always liable to reenter the path of commoditization. Think here of the presence of divination baskets in private and museum collections, and consider the thought-provoking fact that, from the trader's perspective, the de-commoditization and ritual enclaving of the *lipele* is the very condition on which depends its re-commoditization by diversion into the world market, a market in which *authentic* African art is *used* art (Silva 2003). Commoditization theorists remind us that ritual enclaving, bounded, long lasting, and transformational though it is, should not blind us to the fact that the *lipele* is a commodity *in potentia*.

Yet I soon realized that the strength of this approach is also its weakness. In the process of positioning the *lipele* in the circuit of exchange, as it moves in and out of commoditization, commoditization theory is bound to miss the specificity of those actions that occur in the space of ritual. Yet it is here, in the space of ritual, where the *lipele* belongs and spends most of its lifetime, exhibiting an "aura of apartness from the mundane and the common" (Kopytoff 1986:69; see also Pels 1998:98).

It is true that, from above, the process of *lipele* personification appears to corroborate commoditization theory. An oracle made appears to be a commodity unmade. Personification appears to equal de-commoditization. What's more, there appears to be evidence of a strong singularization pull from the time of the birth of the *lipele*: In contrast with ordinary baskets, the making and the delivery of divination baskets are ritualized. Both the basket maker and the diviner must avoid sexual intercourse for as long as the basket is being woven, which may be several months. The diviner must also avoid certain bad foods so that the basket does not lose its potency. Later, the diviner will pay the basket maker for her work, but, as described in Chapter 1, the delivery of the basket must be acted out as if the *lipele* were being "stolen." The act of thievery appears to disguise the basket's commercial origin.

Furthermore, the process of singularization appears to reach completion in the subsequent *lipele* initiation ceremony, described in Chapter 2. By dawn, thanks to the transformative power of ritual, the *lipele* has become a singularity, an oracle, a conduit for Kayongo. Now the *lipele* is said to hear, understand, refuse, demand respect, inspire awe and fear, and take revenge if forgotten. In old age, when its woven body deteriorates and starts malfunctioning, its owner puts it to rest and gives it a proper burial. Sangombe explained: "The basket is the *lipele*'s body, so when the *lipele* dies, we bury it."

Concepts, however, should do justice to the realities that they purportedly elucidate. In the case of divination baskets, the concept of *ex-commodity* is simply too broad and misleading. The *lipele* user avers that once the *lipele* has been ritually activated and personified, it may not revert to the status of an ordinary object and be exchanged for another commodity. This is not only because such is the way it has always been (tradition obliges) but also because the diviner's ancestor (who embodies that tradition) would kill him.

From then on, the source of the *lipele*'s value lies not in economic exchange but in ritual. Why then refer to the *lipele* as an ex-commodity or a potential commodity when its value is no longer determined by economic exchange? Why judge and classify a *lipele* according to its origins and uncertain future? Why reduce it to the sad condition of potentiality? Why not judge the *lipele* for what it is, an oracle?[1]

Our understanding of basket divination is little advanced by conceptualizing the *lipele* as *commodity*, *ex-commodity*, *terminal commodity*, or *enclaved commodity*, and much less by designating the *lipele* as an object. The object is a subject, and the realm where it belongs is not the local pathways and global highways of economic exchange but the carefully bounded enclaves of ritual. The *lipele* is an oracle, and basket divination is a way of knowing and a way of doing, ways that are ritualistic and performative.

Working Tool

That said, the link between divination and economy is not necessarily severed once the diviner "steals" the basket and personifies it. Even if the *lipele* never reenters the commoditization path upon transfer through means told and untold to the hands of an art dealer or a museum curator, it continues to be ontologically perceived as both a subject and an object, a thing of ritual and a thing of economy.

Not all things of economy, however, are necessarily commodities. The diviners I met in Chavuma in the 1990s perceived the *lipele* not as a commodity but as a working tool and divination not as consumption but as production. As they saw it, inasmuch as diviners must use their hands to shake a basket, divining is manual work, comparable to winnowing grain, cultivating the land, or weaving a mat.

Note that the *lipele* continues to play an active role in economic exchange, if only indirectly; no longer a commodity itself, it participates in economic exchange indirectly as the producer of a commodity for which the consulters pay heavy sums—divinatory knowledge.[2] The adult *lipele*, being a person, is carefully protected from commoditization. *She* participates in the local economy directly and indirectly: directly as a worker and indirectly through the product of *her* labor.

In his seminal essay on commoditization, Appadurai urges us to consider the "commodity potential of all things," which in his view means "breaking significantly with the production-dominated Marxian view of the commodity and focusing on its total trajectory from production, through exchange/distribution, to consumption" (1986a:13). Notwithstanding the groundbreaking importance of this theoretical and methodological approach to material things, the people residing in Chavuma in the 1990s opted to foreground the centuries-old understanding of basket divination as production. From above, the biography of the *lipele* may appear to corroborate (de)commoditization theory; on the ground, however, the realm of the economy looks radically different. Now, it is production (in Marx's sense) and not exchange and consumption (in Simmel's sense) that is prioritized. It is here in this culturally framed, historically contextualized understanding of ritual practice as production where the source of the *lipele*'s value properly lies.

It is worth returning momentarily to the ritual of stealing the basket. The ethnography shows that this ritual is best viewed not as a disguise of the commercial origin of the *lipele* (Silva 1999, 2004) but as the reenactment in symbolic form of a contested transfer of power from women to men. It is precisely because the *lipele* as a working tool generates impressive wealth, status, and power that it has always been an arena in which gender politics in south Central Africa are played out.

In his account of the origins of *lipele* divination, Sangombe said clearly, "The first oracle belonged to a woman, not to a man; they quarreled over it." As described in Chapter 2, Sangombe explained that the first oracle ever known to humankind belonged to Nyakweleka, a Lunda woman who divined with a pestle in Musumba until the day her Luvale husband, Sakweleka, took it from her. Similarly, chieftainship in Musumba belonged to a woman named Luweji until the day her Luba husband, Chibinda Ilunga, usurped it. In both cases, women lose power to foreign men in the institutional context of wedlock, the thing usurped mutating into something else—the pestle into a *lipele*, and the egalitarian political system of the matrilineal *tubungu* chiefs into the hierarchical one of the patrilineal Mwachiyavwa kings.[3] Regeneration comes from elsewhere, and otherness is a source of both vitality and worry. This contested transfer of power from women to men is best encapsulated in a Luvale proverb often quoted in formulaic speeches: *Uta wapwile wapwevo lunga amunyangawo* (The bow belonged to a woman, and a man took it from her).

It is true that in ideology, if not in practice, the relationship between men and women in south Central Africa is more often described as complementary. During the ritual in Kalwiji, for example, Sangombe referred to the old and new baskets as his two wives, saying that the new basket was his favorite and that the time had come to empty and bury the old one. Diviners see their baskets as their wives, fertile women who generate life. Their union with the baskets, appositely woven with the coiling technique and decorated with pestle motifs, evokes the ideological principle of gender complementarity, recurring not only in the legendary relationship between Sakweleka and Nyakweleka but also in the historical relationships that diviners form with vaNyaminenge, meaning their wives of flesh and bone, and the living women who wove their baskets. In theory, if not in practice, women produce *lipele* oracles for men and help them ritually and otherwise on the expectation that men put the oracles to work and share their earnings with them.

Yet the *lipele* is symbolically described as a source of conflict between men and women. Sakweleka and Nyakweleka quarreled over the *lipele*, and in the end Sakweleka "convinced" his wife to put aside her pestle and weave a *lipele* for him. Could one see in Sakutemba's refusal of the status of Nyaminenge to his wife an extreme contemporary expression of a centuries-old process of political encroachment? Sakutemba did not engage in open ritualized quarreling with basket maker Pezo—an ethnic other to him, like Nyakweleka and Luweji were to their respective husbands, Sakweleka and Ilunga—but the double-edged nature of their relationship was given symbolic expression in occasional sarcasm, nervous humor, and the culminating act of stealing.

Note that the *lipele* is deemed worth stealing not because it is perceived as a commodity, a thing exchangeable in a one-time transaction for another thing or money, profitable as this transaction might turn out to be, but because it is a bow, an endless source of wealth, status, and political power. The *lipele* is a means of production.

Way of Living

In *Early Writings*, Marx wrote: "To say that a man is a *corporeal*, living, real, sensuous, objective being with natural powers means that he has *real, sensuous objects* as the objects of his being and of his vital expression, or that he can only *express* his life in real, sensuous objects. . . . To be sensuous is to *suffer* (to be subjected to the actions of another). Man as an objective, sensuous being is therefore a *suffering* being, and because he feels his suffering, he is a *passionate* being" (1975:390, quoted in Pietz 1993:144; Marx's emphasis). The diviners I met in Chavuma were passionate in Marx's sense. They saw themselves as "living, real, sensuous" men with bodily and social needs, their prestigious, well-paid profession serving as a means to satisfy them. For them, to divine was to labor and to suffer in the double sense that Kayongo inflicts pain on diviners and that life in exile is painful. Because they were "subjected to the actions of another," spiritual or human, timeless or historical, all they could do was to suffer along intrepidly and always to work with a passion. They hoped to remain healthy, have the strength to shake their baskets, and be wise with their earnings. They drew great pleasure from watching their possessions, and they liked to think that their fields, cattle, and women would thrive and multiply, attracting relatives from far and wide to their burgeoning, full-of-life villages. This was the reward of their toil and labor.

For those living in Chavuma in the 1990s, there was nothing paradoxical, unsophisticated, or dull about viewing basket divination as work and labor; quite the contrary, basket divination's economic value—made possible by its social recognition as a legitimate and powerful way of getting to know and do things—became instrumental in the diviners' struggle to remake life in exile. Diviners may have arrived in Chavuma as destitute and disoriented as the other Angolan refugees and they may have had to farm as all villagers, and, like them, perceive their quotidian as a struggle, but their larger and populous villages, the respect they inspired in others (including the Zambians), and their self-confidence spoke volumes. The *lipele* became their alter ego, their lifelong companion, their tool that facilitated action.

I do not think that the definition of the *lipele* as a tool brings us any closer to its essence than its definition as an object, subject, fetish, or ex-commodity. Such definition, however, does suggest that past and present intersect in basket divination, a centuries-old cultural practice, traditional by all definitions, becoming a vital part of a contemporary existence where people live under objectifying threats—threats that are, once again, old and new: fear, disorientation, pain, illness, poverty, isolation, displacement, and death.

Basket divination is not an expression of the fetishistic mind, bound to express its fancies in concrete form. The process of personifying an object and objectifying a diviner within ritual reflects back the passionate struggle by diviners and consulters to achieve de-objectification outside ritual. They both see themselves as sufferers and perceive their situation as an impasse, a crisis with a resolution that involves object-mediated spiritual intervention. For the consulters, this resolution becomes expressed as learning the truth (as described in Chapter 3); for the Angolan diviners, it becomes expressed as making a living (as described in Chapter 1). Existentially, then, the historically contingent understanding of basket divination as work and labor is equivalent to its universal understanding in south Central Africa as a way of knowing.

MacGaffey suggests that "the *minkisi* of traditional Kongo, having been defined as persons, returned the favor by defining the social status of their owners" (1990:54). I would say that divination baskets, in addition to granting the diviners a similar social favor, allow them as well as their clients to de-objectify themselves. Is not the personification of material objects, as Jackson suggests (2004), a gift that humans offer material objects in the hope of receiving social and existential advantages in return?

The view that *lipele* divination is a way of knowing, a way of doing, and a way of working and laboring is incomplete. In divination, people attempt to explain life, do things through ritual, and earn a livelihood all at once and with no sense of fragmentation. For them, divination is "a definite form of activity . . . a definite form of expressing their life, a definite *mode of life* on their part. As individuals express their life, so they are" (Marx and Engels 1976:31, emphasis in original).

Notes

Introduction

1. All vernacular terms used hereafter, unless otherwise stated, are written in Luvale, the language spoken by the Luvale people, or the *Valuvale,* often referred to in the literature as Lwena. In Chavuma, the Zambian district where I conducted two years of fieldwork, this language is also spoken by other closely related groups, such as the Chokwe, Luchazi, and Mbunda. I use the Luvale spelling adopted in Zambia, but I have flattened all aspirated consonants (*ph*, for example, appears as *p*). All Luvale terms used recurrently in this book are listed in the Glossary.

2. For other cognitive approaches to anthropomorphism, see Boyer 1996 and Guthrie 1993.

3. The somatization of trauma has been studied in psychoanalysis by such authors as Brett (1996), Brody (1994), Friedman and Jaranson (1994), Orley (1994), and Parker (1996:268-69).

4. Several authors have underscored this existential and pragmatist dimension of divination, among them Graw (2006, 2009), Shaw (1985, 1991), and Whyte (1991, 1997).

5. For the influx of Angolans into Zambia during colonialism, see, for example, Cabrita 1954; Mitchell 1954; Powles 2000:7-8; and White 1949b, 1960:3.

6. For information on the Angolan wars, from the liberation struggle in the 1960s to the cease-fire in 2002, see Birmingham 1992, 2006; Brinkman 2003; Chabal 2002; Chabal and Vidal 2008; Ciment 1997; Davidson 1972:251-75; Guimarães 1998, Messiant 1998; Newitt 2008; and Pélissier 1974.

7. For the resettlement of Angolan refugees in Zambia, see Barrett 1998; Hansen 1976, 1979a, 1979b, 1990; Mijere 1995; Powles 2000; and Wilson 1986.

8. These figures refer to Chavuma subdistrict, that is, to the wards located on the east bank of the Zambezi River. Chavuma became a district in 1997 and was expanded to include the wards located on the west bank (see Annex 3, "Households and Population Distribution by Ward, Constituency, District and Province," Central Statistical Office 2001).

9. For similar spirits reported elsewhere in Africa, such as the *zar, hauka,* and *masabe,* see for example, Boddy 1989; Kramer 1993/1987; and Stoller 1989a, 1995.

10. In the early 1990s, Manuel Jordán met a diviner in Kabompo, North-Western province, Zambia, whose divination basket included a small plastic toy soldier that

stood for a person killed during the Angolan civil wars or a form of affliction caused by an ancestor who died in combat (1996:264). In Chavuma, I never came across a divination basket containing a comparable article.

11. I thank Michael Jackson for helping me shape this argument.

12. For a general overview of important sociocultural and historical aspects of the Upper Zambezi and south Central Africa, see Hudson 1935; McCulloch 1951; Pritchett 2001; Redinha 1958; Reefe 1983; Vansina 1966; Wastiau 2000; and White 1949b, 1960.

Chapter 1

A portion of this chapter appeared previously, in a different form, in Sónia Silva, "The Birth of a Divination Basket," in *Chokwe! Art and Initiation among Chokwe and Related Peoples,* ed. Manuel Jordán (Munich: Prestel, 1998), 141-51.

1. All names of individuals and residential areas within the district of Chavuma are pseudonyms.

2. Elsewhere, I translated the Luvale term *mwivwi* as "advance fee" or "first payment" (Silva 1998:141-52). I now believe that the term *deposit* is a better translation, for it evokes both the initial payment of a cost and the creation of a bond or relationship of trust between diviner and basket maker. Diviner Sanjamba told me, "The diviner gives a small deposit to the basket maker so that she knows that she has been given work, so that she says to herself, 'When I finish making this basket, the diviner will come and pay me for my work.' She says this because he has already given her the deposit."

3. *Mufu* is a dead person whose life force (*mwono*) has already departed and whose body is not yet decomposed. The physical corpse is called *chivimbi* (White 1948a:146-56). Kakoma's statement that the basket is the corpse of the late diviner implies that this basket will be animated through contact with Kayongo, a spiritual manifestation of the late diviner, in the course of a ritual ceremony.

4. Between September 1995 and January 1997 the average exchange rate was 1,000 *kwachas* to one US dollar. In Chavuma, a large chicken, for example, sold for 2,000 *kwachas*, and a good *chitenge* wrapping cloth sold for 4,800 *kwachas*. For people with little access to cash, 10,000 *kwachas* was (and still is) a significant amount.

5. On the link between speech and the act of striking the earth or another material base, see, for example, Keane 1998:20; Livingstone 1857:488; and MacGaffey 2000:104-5.

6. Clans, or *miyachi*, are highly dispersed and noncorporate groups shared by the Luvale and related peoples. For a discussion of the origin and significance of these social groups, twelve in number, see White 1957.

7. This contradicts fisherman Kakoma's statement that a *lipele* is buried with the corpse of its owner, as well as Merran McCulloch's remark that "at the death of the diviner his basket is destroyed" (1951:82).

8. I was told that this salt came from Katumbela (Katombelo in Luvale), a town about fifteen miles from Benguela, on the Atlantic coast. On the importance of salt in the regional trade, see Childs 1949:201; Papstein 1978:242; Sangambo 1979:78; and Schindler 1986:74. For a discussion of the role played by the Ovimbundu in linking the

Upper Zambezi to the Atlantic Coast during the caravan trade, see Papstein 1978:42 and von Oppen 1994:53-56.

9. See, for example, Bastin 1988, de Boeck and Devisch 1994, Rodrigues de Areia 1985, and Turner 1975/1961.

10. Don Ihde claims, consequently, that touch too is a distance sense, contrary to empiricism (1979:7).

11. The English word "labor" also evokes the pains of childbirth, a sense that is compatible with the Luvale idea that the divinatory work—the revelation of knowledge—causes physical pain to the diviner.

Chapter 2

1. The events described in these chiefly epics represent long, complex historical processes of alliance and conflict between different groups. Names such as Luweji, Chinyama, and so on, represent political titles passed down through generations (de Heusch 1982:10; Miller 1972:551, 570-74). For a detailed account of the Luvale chiefly epic described here, see Sangambo 1979; for the Lunda and Chokwe versions of the same epic, see Dias de Carvalho 1890:58-73; de Heusch 1982:144-51; Lima 1971:42-50; and McCulloch 1951:9-12.

2. It is true that in 1938, following three decades of forced subordination to the Lozi kingdom, the Luvale (as well as the Lunda-Shinde) presented a written document to the British MacDonnell Commission of Inquiry, demonstrating in great detail their kinship with the Northern Lunda king. In 1971, the Luvale and the Lunda-Shinde again presented their history in writing, this time to an inquiring commission constituted by President Kenneth Kaunda to ascertain their opposing claims to Chavuma (Papstein 1989). These, however, are historical and political struggles spearheaded by members of intellectual elites, such Mose Kaputungu Sangambo, author of *The History of the Luvale People and their Chieftainship* (1979).

3. There was some disagreement about the kind of oracle this was. One diviner spoke of a calabash bowl (*suhwa*) and explained the switch to a woven basket by pointing out that calabashes crack easily, being remarkably less durable than baskets made with tough *kenge* roots. It occurred to me that this version of history possibly echoes the fact that the Luvale word *lipele* denotes both the divining basket and a large calabash. This version also suggests the historical link between the Luvale and the peoples living in the southwest region of the Democratic Republic of the Congo, where the Luba still use a gourd filled with small articles for divining (Roberts 2000:63). Others in southeast Angola use calabash bowls with a perforated rim and a woven section on top (see, for example, Delachaux 1946a). Most diviners in Chavuma, however, disagreed upfront with the calabash-bowl theory.

4. In several sources, Nyakapamba Musopa is identified as Luweji lwaKonde, Ilunga's wife (Martins 1993:145; White 1949b:34, 1960:45). I was told in Chavuma that she was a *kabungu* female chief who left Inkalanyi after Chinguli's departure, in the company of the following individuals: her consort (*mukwetunga*) Kavungu; the senior adviser to the chief (*mulopwe* or *ngambela*) Muvumbula; and two of her daughters, Ndumba and Tembo.

This information agrees with Sangambo's history, which claims that Nyakapamba Musopanama (*sic*) and her consort Samwana Kalunda (*sic*) followed in the path of Chinguli, their children Sumba and Jembo (*sic*) becoming Chokwe chiefs (1979:31).

5. Kinship *mahamba* differ from other, newer *mahamba*, said to travel with the wind. For a discussion of the meaning and types of *mahamba*, see Lima 1971:79-90; Martins 1993:111; Rodrigues de Areia 1985:419-40; Wastiau 2000; and White 1949a.

6. I am echoing here Austin's concepts of "illocutionary force" and "illocutionary acts" (1975). Numerous anthropologists have drawn on these concepts—for example, Bloch 1974; Connerton 1989:58-60; and Tambiah 1968, 1979:141-42.

7. The vervet monkey (*soko* in Luvale) is the *Cercopithecus aethiops*. The yellow baboon (*hundu*, *pombo*, or *puya* in Luvale) is the *Papio cynocephalus* (White and Ansell 1966:182).

8. "The tree stump in the path hurts ten toes," or *Kambunji kamujila kamana kumi lyaminwe*, is a metaphorical reference to the power of diviners. Kashinde Kamujila Kamana Kumi Lyaminwe (*kashinde* is a hump of sod) is also the praise name of a celebrated Angolan diviner who lived in the 1900s.

9. This Angolan francolin, *Pternistis afer* (Horton 1953:253), is known for the redness of its bare throat, which contrasts with the whiteness of its forehead and superciliary and moustachial stripes extending down the throat's sides (Mackworth-Praed and Grant 1962:221-22). These authors classify the *Pternistis afer* as a spurfowl, outside the category of francolins proper.

10. The *mukondo* has been identified as both the red mongoose, or *Galerella bocagei* (Horton 1953:131), and the dwarf mongoose, or *Helogale parvula* (White and Ansell 1966:182). The coat of the *Galerella bocagei* is ocherous in color (Hill and Carter 1941:128). The dwarf mongoose's coloring ranges from yellowish and reddish to dark brown and black (Kingdon 1997:243).

11. The mannikin bird, a small weaver-finch known in Luvale as *kajilili*, belongs to the genera *Lonchura* (Horton 1953:89).

12. Semi, the fertile one, may be a reference to Ilunga's second wife, Kamongalwaza, who in the Luvale tradition, as mentioned, bore him three children. Mumba, the childless one, may be Luweji, Ilunga's first wife, who in the same tradition is said to have had no children (Sangambo 1979:10-11).

13. This arboreal bird, *nduwa* in Luvale, is also called Plantain-Eater or Lady Ross's Turaco (*Musophaga rossae* [Horton 1953:238]). It is wholly blue-black and violet in color except for crimson in the wings and chest (Mackworth-Praed and Grant 1962:432). For a description of the lourie's symbolic importance, see Rodrigues de Areia 1985:310-12.

14. See, for example, Bastin 1988:22-25; de Boeck and Devisch 1994:113-15; Hauenstein 1961:124-26; Martins 1993:138-49; Rodrigues de Areia 1985:81-87; Tucker 1940:175-78; and Turner 1975/1961:247-68.

15. The expression *chikungulu kaliveya* evokes the proverb *Chikungulu kaliveya muhita ufuku waunene* (The eagle owl never misses its prey no matter how long the night).

Chapter 3

1. The Luvale distinguish between epilepsy in children, *lyavanyike* or *kalekale*, and epilepsy in adults, *chikonya*. "Doctor" is my translation for the Luvale word *chimbanda*.

2. For a discussion of the impact of Christianity, colonialism, and postcolonialism on African matrilineal societies, some of them Zambian, see, for example, Cliggett 2005; Crehan 1994, 1997; Douglas 1969; Gough 1961; Holy 1986; Poewe 1978a, 1978b, 1978c; and Schapera 1947.

3. Several authors have studied the interactional and performative aspects of divinatory rituals; see, for example, Parkin 1991, Shaw 1991, Werbner 1989, Whyte 1991, Wilce 2001, and Winkelman and Peek 2004.

4. *Ngele* is the same as *muhale*, identified by White and Ansell as the sun squirrel (*Heliosciurus gambianus*), an arboreal and diurnal rodent (1966:182). The scientific term for the night-ape, *katoto* in Luvale, is *Galago senegalensis*. Night-apes, better known as lesser bush babies, are nocturnal, arboreal feeders that sleep during the daytime in dense vegetation, tree forks, hollow trees, and old bird nests (Kingdon 1997:102).

5. The *mupepe* tree (singular of *mipepe*), known for the hardness of its wood, represents a man; the *muli* (singular of *mili*), known for oozing out white latex, represents a woman. The *mupepe* is the *Hymenocardia mollis* (White 1961:2); and the *muli*, also named *muulya*, is the *Diplorhynchus mossambicensis* (White 1962:2).

6. Mutondo used the word *lifuchi* to denote a tree seed that in the *lipele* jargon is called Chifuchi, or Place. For a list of possible scientific identifications of the tree that bears such seeds, see Rodrigues de Areia 1985:149.

7. For a discussion of lineage and Atlantic slavery in the Upper Zambezi and elsewhere in Central Africa, see Douglas 1964; Lovejoy 1983; Miers and Kopytoff 1977; Miller 1981, 1988; Papstein 1978; Von Oppen 1994; and White 1957.

8. Huntsmanship (*unyanga*) is represented in Mutondo's basket by a wooden, miniature gun (*uta*). In other divination baskets, this article consists of a miniature bow because the word *uta* denotes both a bow (*uta wamanana*) and a shotgun or cap gun (*uta wachifwifwi* or *uta wakanjonja*) (Horton 1953:376). According to Sapasa, the ancestor of Chinyama's wife probably owned a flintlock (*mbanja*), the most common rifle available in those days.

9. On the importance of the materialization and visualization of one's predicament in divination, see Young 1977:192-93, 197; see also Jordán 1996:228; Tedlock 2001; Winkelman and Peek 2004:18; and Zeitlyn 2001:230.

10. Another version of this song says, *Kandemba waya, shili / Shili yaupite* (Kandemba died, envy / Envy of wealth).

11. Drawing on different disciplines and theoretical paradigms, several authors have argued that divination is both analytical and synthetical, this duality, or rather the integration of this duality in its multiple configurations, being its defining feature as a way of knowing. See Fernandez 1991, Graw 2009, Parkin 1991, Peek 1991a, and Tedlock 2001, 2006.

Conclusion

1. In south Central Africa, women and divination baskets (also female) are onto-logically ambiguous in similar ways. Women are given in marriage to men in exchange for the bride-price (*litemo*), an economic transaction that in times past, much like the *lipele* today, appears to have been ritually enacted as theft or, more precisely, abduction. Women and divination baskets share not only a high degree of ontological ambivalence, being now subjects, now objects; they also share the important fact that, notwithstanding that ambivalence, they are better described as "persons" rather than "commodities."

2. Appadurai would call divinatory knowledge a "terminal commodity," a commodity with one single journey from production to consumption (1986a:23).

3. The Luvale, however, have remained a relatively egalitarian and strongly matrilin-eal people who enthrone female chiefs (Cabrita 1954:46). See also Wim van Binsbergen's historical and structuralist analysis of the transfer of power from women to men among the Nkoya of Kaoma, Zambia (1987), and Manuela Palmeirim's discussion of the principles of egalitarianism and hierarchy in the Northern Lunda kingship ideology (1998).

Glossary

Recurrent Luvale Words

chimbanda (pl. *vimbanda*)	doctor; herbalist; ritual expert
Ilunga	Luba hunter who married Luweji
Kayongo	divination *lihamba*
kenge (lukenge) (pl. *jikenge*)	root from the *mukenge* tree used in basket making
kukombela	to invoke the spirits
kumba (pl. *jikumba*)	basket used for storing and carrying the *lipele*
kusekula	to shake the divination basket
kutaha	to divine
kutunga	to make or build
kuzata	to work
kuzachisa	to use
lihamba (hamba) (pl. *mahamba*)	ancestral manifestation; material representation of an ancestor
lipele (pl. *mapele*)	divination basket
lukano (pl. *jikano*)	metallic bracelet inherited from an ancestor
Luweji	chiefly title; Ilunga's first wife
lwalo (pl. *jilwalo*)	winnowing basket
mbango (pl. *jimbango*)	coiled basket

milimo (pl. *milimo*)   labor (*mulimo*, the singular form, is no longer
                               used)

mukakutaha   diviner
    (pl. *vakakutaha*)

mukandumba   witch or wizard
    (pl. *vakandumba*)

mukenge (pl. *mikenge*)   tree (*Combretum zeyheri*); see *kenge*

mukula (pl. *mikula*)   bloodwood tree (*Ptecarpus angolensis*)

muloji (pl. *valoji*)   witch or sorcerer

munenge (pl. *minenge*)   bloodwood pole used as divination shrine

musambo (pl. *misambo*)   divination rattle shaken during invocation

muyombo (pl. *miyombo*)   tree (*Lannea stuhlmanni*) used for invoking and
                               appeasing the ancestors

mwĭvwĭ (pl. *mivwi*)   arrow; deposit

ngombo (pl. *jingombo*)   material oracle

ngula   red clay

Nyakweleka   woman who divined with a pestle in Musumba;
                               Sakweleka's wife

Nyaminenge   title of the diviner's senior wife

pelo (lupelo) (pl. *jipelo*)   divination article; powerful organic substance

pemba   white clay

ponde (pl. *jiponde*)   sudden violent death; disease caused by an
                               ancestor who died in this way

pumba (pl. *vapumba*)   divination apprentice

Sakweleka   the first *lipele* diviner; Nyakweleka's husband

somo (pl. *jisomo*)   horn used by diviners to attract clients

tewa (pl. *vatewa*)   consulter (the diviner's client)

Works Cited

Allen, Tim, ed. 1996. *Search of Cool Ground: War, Flight, and Homecoming in Northeast Africa*. Trenton, N.J.: Africa World Press.

Appadurai, Arjun. 1986a. Introduction: Commodities and the Politics of Value. In *The Social Life of Things: Commodities in Cultural Perspective*, edited by Arjun Appadurai, 3-64. Cambridge: Cambridge University Press.

Appadurai, Arjun, ed. 1986b. *The Social Life of Things: Commodities in Cultural Perspective*. Cambridge: Cambridge University Press.

Applebaum, Herbert. 1992. *The Concept of Work: Ancient, Medieval, and Modern*. New York: State University of New York Press.

Arendt, Hannah. 1958. *The Human Condition*. Chicago: University of Chicago Press.

Armstrong, Robert Plant. 1971. *Affecting Presence: An Essay in Humanistic Anthropology*. Urbana: University of Illinois Press.

Austin, John L. 1975. *How to Do Things with Words*. Oxford: Oxford University Press.

Baker, K. 1988. *Minimalism: Art of Circumstance*. New York: Abbeville Press.

Barrett, Michael. 1998. *Tuvosena: "Let's Go Everybody." Identity and Ambition among Angolan Refugees in Zambia*. Uppsala: Department of Cultural Anthropology and Ethnology, Uppsala University.

Bastin, Marie-Louise. 1959. Ngombo: Notes sur les instruments de divination employés dans le District de la Lunda en Angola. *Congo-Tervuren* 5 (4):100-106.

———. 1961. *Art décoratif tshokwe*. Lisbon: Companhia de Diamantes de Angola.

———. 1988. A propos du panier divinatoire tshokwe. *Arts d'Afrique Noire* 68:19-27.

Bauman, Richard, and Charles Briggs. 1990. Poetics and Performance as Critical Perspectives on Language and Social Life. *Annual Review of Anthropology* 19:59-88.

Baumann, Hermann. 1935. *Lunda: Bei Bauern und Jägern in Inner-Angola*. Berlin: Würfel Verlag Berlin.

Beattie, John. 1964. Divination in Bunyoro, Uganda. *Sociologus* 14:44-62.

———. 1966. Ritual and Social Change. *Man* 1 (1):60-73.

Birmingham, David. 1992. *Frontline Nationalism in Angola & Mozambique*. London: James Currey.

———. 2006. *Empire in Africa: Angola and Its Neighbors*. Athens: Ohio University Research in International Studies with Ohio University Press.

Blier, Suzanne Preston. 1993. Truth and Seeing: Magic, Custom and Fetish in Art History. In *Africa and the Disciplines,* edited by Robert Bates, 139-66. Chicago: University of Chicago Press.

———. 1995. *African Vodun: Art, Psychology, and Power.* Chicago: University of Chicago Press.

Bloch, Maurice. 1974. Symbols, Song, Dance and Features of Articulation: Is Religion an Extreme Form of Traditional Authority? *Archives Européennes de Sociologie* 15:55-81.

Boddy, Janice. 1989. *Wombs and Alien Spirits: Women, Men, and the Zar Cult in Northern Sudan.* Madison: University of Wisconsin Press.

———. 1994. Spirit Possession Revisited: Beyond Instrumentality. *Annual Review of Anthropology* 23:407-34.

Boyer, Pascal. 1996. What Makes Anthropomorphism Natural: Intuitive Ontology and Cultural Representations. *Journal of the Royal Anthropological Institute* 2:83-97.

Brett, Amelia. 1996. Testimonies of War Trauma in Uganda. In *In Search of Cool Ground: War, Flight, and Homecoming in Northeast Africa,* edited by Tim Allen, 278-92. Trenton, N.J.: Africa World Press.

Brett-Smith, Sarah C. 1994. *The Making of Bamana Sculpture: Creativity and Gender.* Cambridge: Cambridge University Press.

Brinkman, Inge. 2003. War, Witches and Traitors: Cases from the MPLA's Eastern Front in Angola (1966-1975). *Journal of African History* 44:303-25.

Brody, Eugene. 1994. The Mental Health and Well-Being of Refugees: Issues and Directions. In *Amidst Peril and Pain: The Mental Health and Well-Being of the World's Refugees,* edited by Anthony J. Marsella, Thomas Bornemann, Solvig Ekblad, and John Orley, 57-68. Washington, D.C.: American Psychological Association.

Cabrita, Carlos L. Antunes. 1954. *Em terras de luenas: Breve estudo sobre os usos e costumes da tribo luena.* Lisbon: Agência Geral do Ultramar.

Cameron, Verney Lovett. 1877. *Across Africa.* New York: Harper.

Carrithers, Michael, Steven Collins, and Steven Lukes, eds. 1985. *The Category of the Person: Anthropology, Philosophy, History.* Cambridge: Cambridge University Press.

Casey, Edward S. 1987. *Remembering: A Phenomenological Study.* Bloomington: Indiana University Press.

Central Statistical Office. 2001. *2000 Census of Population and Housing: Preliminary Report.* (Electronic file). Lusaka: Central Statistical Office.

Chabal, Patrick, ed. 2002. *A History of Postcolonial Lusophone Africa.* Bloomington: Indiana University Press.

Chabal, Patrick, and Nuno Vidal, eds. 2008. *Angola: The Weight of History.* New York: Columbia University Press.

Cheke Cultural Writers, The. 1994. *The History and Cultural Life of the Mbunda Speaking Peoples,* edited by Robert Papstein. Lusaka: Cheke Cultural Writers Association.

Childs, Gladwyn M. 1949. *Umbundu Kinship and Character*. Oxford: Oxford University Press.

Ciment, James. 1997. *Angola and Mozambique: Post-Colonial Wars in Southern Africa*. New York: Facts on File.

Clarence-Smith, William Gervase. 1983. Capital Accumulation and Class Formation in Angola. In *History of Central Africa*, edited by D. Birmingham and P. M. Martin, 2:163-99. London: Longman.

Cliggett, Lisa. 2005. *Grains from Grass: Aging, Gender, and Famine in Rural Africa*. Ithaca, N.Y.: Cornell University Press.

Connerton, Paul. 1989. *How Societies Remember*. Cambridge: Cambridge University Press.

Crehan, Kate. 1994. Land, Labour and Gender: Matriliny in 1980s Rural Zambia. Paper presented at the meeting of the African Studies Association, Toronto.

———. 1997. *The Fractured Community: Landscapes of Power and Gender in Ritual Zambia*. Berkeley: University of California Press.

Davidson, Basil. 1972. *In the Eye of the Storm*. New York: Doubleday.

Davis, John. 1992. The Anthropology of Suffering. *Journal of Refugee Studies* 5 (2):149-61.

De Boeck, Filip. 1991. Therapeutic Efficacy and Consensus among the Aluund of South-Western Zaire. *Africa* 61 (2):160-85.

———. 1993. Symbolic and Diachronic Study of Inter-Cultural Therapeutic and Divinatory Roles among the Aluund ("Lunda") and Chokwe in the Upper Kwaango (South Western Zaire). *Afrika Focus* 9 (1–2):73–104.

———. 1995. Bodies of Remembrance: Knowledge, Experience and the Growing of Memory in Luunda Ritual Performance. In *Rites and Ritualisation*, edited by Georges Thines and Luc de Heusch, 113-38. Paris: J. Vrin.

De Boeck, Filip, and René Devisch. 1994. Ndembu, Luunda and Yaka Divination Compared: From Representation and Social Engineering to Embodiment and Worldmaking. *Journal of Religion in Africa* 24 (2):98-133.

De Heusch, Luc. 1971. *Pourquoi l'épouser?* Paris: Gallimard.

———. 1982. *The Drunken King or the Origin of the State*. Bloomington: Indiana University Press.

Delachaux, Théodore. 1946a. Méthodes et instruments de divination en Angola. *Acta Tropica* 3 (1):48-72.

———. 1946b. Méthodes et instruments de divination en Angola (suite). *Acta Tropica* 3 (2):138-47.

Devisch, René. 1985. Perspectives on Divination in Contemporary Sub-Saharan Africa. In *Theoretical Explorations in African Religion*, edited by W. van Binsbergen and M. Schoffeleers, 50-83. London: Routledge and Kegan Paul.

———. 2004. Yaka Divination: Acting Out the Memory of Society's Life-Spring. In *Divination and Healing: Potent Visions*, edited by Michael Winkelman and Philip M. Peek, 243-63. Tucson: University of Arizona Press.

Dias de Carvalho, Henrique Augusto. 1890. *Ethnographia e história tradicional dos povos da Lunda*. Lisbon: Imprensa Nacional.

Douglas, Mary. 1964. Matriliny and Pawnship in Central Africa. *Africa* 34 (4):301-13.

——. 1969. Is Matriliny Doomed in Africa? In *Man in Africa,* edited by Mary Douglas and P. M. Kaberry, 121-36. London: Routledge.

DuBois, John W. 1992. Meaning Without Intention: Lessons from Divination. In *Responsibility and Evidence in Oral Discourse*, edited by J. H. Hill and J. T. Irvine, 48-71. Cambridge: Cambridge University Press.

Edie, James M. 1963. Expression and Metaphor. *Philosophy and Phenomenological Research* 23 (4):538-61.

Ellen, Roy. 1988. Fetishism. *Man* 23 (2):213-35.

——. 1990. Nuaulu Sacred Shields: The Reproduction of Things or the Reproduction of Images? *Etnofoor* 3 (1):5.

Evans-Pritchard, E. 1976. *Witchcraft, Oracles and Magic among the Azande*. Oxford: Clarendon Press.

Fabian, Johannes. 1983. *Time and the Other: How Anthropology Makes Its Object*. New York: Columbia University Press.

Fernandez, James W. 1991. Afterword. In *African Divination Systems: Ways of Knowing*, edited by Philip M. Peek, 213-22. Bloomington: Indiana University Press.

Friedman, Matthew, and James Jaranson. 1994. The Applicability of the Posttraumatic Stress Disorder Concept to Refugees. In *Amidst Peril and Pain: The Mental Health and Well-Being of the World's Refugees*, edited by Anthony J. Marsella, Thomas Bornemann, Solvig Ekblad, and John Orley, 207-28. Washington, D.C.: American Psychological Association.

Gell, Alfred. 1998. *Art and Agency: An Anthropological Theory*. Oxford: Clarendon Press.

Goffman, Erving. 1981. *Forms of Talk*. Philadelphia: University of Pennsylvania Press.

Gough, Kathleen. 1961. The Modern Disintegration of Matrilineal Descent Groups. In *Matrilineal Kinship*, edited by David M. Schneider and Kathleen Gough, 631-52. Berkeley: University of California Press.

Graw, Knut. 2006. Locating *Nganiyo*: Divination as Intentional Space. *Journal of Religion in Africa* 36 (1):78-119.

——. 2009. Beyond Expertise: Reflections on Specialist Agency and the Autonomy of the Divinatory Ritual Process. *Africa* 79 (1):92-109.

Guimarães, Fernando Andresen. 1998. *The Origins of the Angolan Civil War: Foreign Intervention and Domestic Political Conflict*. New York: St. Martin's Press.

Guthrie, S. 1993. *Faces in the Clouds*. New York: Oxford University Press.

Hansen, Art. 1976. Once the Running Stops: The Social and Economic Incorporation of Angolan Refugees into Zambian Border Villages. Ph.D. diss., Cornell University.

——. 1979a. Once the Running Stops: Assimilation of Angolan Refugees into Zambian Border Villages. *Disasters* 3 (4):369-74.

———. 1979b. Managing Refugees: Zambia's Response to Angolan Refugees 1966-1977. *Disasters* 3 (4):375-80.

———. 1982. Self-Settled Rural Refugees in Africa: The Case of Angolans in Zambian Villages. In *Involuntary Migration and Settlement*, edited by Art Hansen and A. Oliver-Smith, 13-35. Boulder, Colo.: Westview Press.

———. 1990. *Refugee Self-Settlement versus Settlement on Government Schemes: The Long-Term Consequences for Security, Integration and Economic Development of Angolan Refugees (1966-1989) in Zambia*. Geneva: United Nations Research Institute.

Hansen, Art, and A. Oliver-Smith, eds. 1982. *Involuntary Migration and Settlement*. Boulder, Colo.: Westview Press.

Harris, Grace G. 1989. Concepts of Individual, Self, and Person in Description and Analysis. *American Anthropologist* 91 (3):599-612.

Harvey, Virginia. 1986. *The Techniques of Basketry*. Seattle: Washington University Press.

Hauenstein, Alfred. 1961. La corbeille aux osselets divinatoires des tchokwe (Angola). *Anthropos* 56:114-57.

———. 1985. La corbeille divinatoire des ovimbundu d'Angola. *Bulletin du Musée d'Ethnographie de Genève* 27:65-79.

———. 1988. Culte des mahamba chez les tshokwe. *Bulletin du Musée d'Ethnographie de Genève* 30:97-115.

Hill, John Eric, and T. Donald Carter. 1941. The Mammals of Angola, Africa. *Bulletin of the American Museum of Natural History* 78:1-213.

Holy, Ladislav. 1986. *Strategies and Norms in a Changing Matrilineal Society: Descent, Succession and Inheritance among the Toka of Zambia*. Cambridge: Cambridge University Press.

Horton, A. E. 1953. *A Dictionary of Luvale*. El Monte, Calif.: Rahn Brothers.

Horton, Robin. 1964. Kalabari Diviners and Oracles. *Odu: University of Ife Journal of African Studies* 1 (1):3-16.

———. 1993/1967. African Traditional Thought and Western Science. In *Patterns of Thought in Africa and the West: Essays on Magic, Religion and Science*, 197-258. Cambridge: Cambridge University Press.

Hoskins, Janet. 1998. *Biographical Objects: How Things Tell the Stories of People's Lives*. London: Routledge.

Hudson, R. S. 1935. The Human Geography of Balovale District, Northern Rhodesia. *Journal of the Royal Anthropological Institute of Great Britain and Ireland* 65:235-66.

Ihde, Don. 1979. *Technics and Praxis*. Dordrecht, Holland: D. Reidel.

Jackson, Michael. 1989. *Paths Toward a Clearing: Radical Empiricism and Ethnographic Inquiry*. Bloomington: Indiana University Press.

———. 1996. Introduction: Phenomenology, Radical Empiricism and Anthropological Critique. In *Things as They Are: New Directions in Phenomenological Anthropology*, edited by Michael Jackson, 1-50. Bloomington: Indiana University Press.

——. 1998. *Minima Ethnographica: Intersubjectivity and the Anthropological Project*. Chicago: University of Chicago Press.

——. 2004. Prefácio to *Vidas em jogo: Cestas de adivinhação e refugiados angolanos na Zâmbia*, by Sónia Silva. Lisbon: Instituto de Ciências Sociais.

Jacobson-Widding, Anita. 1979. *Red-White-Black as a Mode of Thought: A Study of Triadic Classification by Colours in the Ritual Symbolism and Cognitive Thought of the Peoples of the Lower Congo*. Uppsala: University of Stockholm.

James, Wendy. 1997. The Names of Fear: Memory, History, and the Ethnography of Feeling among Uduk Refugees. *Journal of the Royal Anthropological Institute* 3 (1):115-33.

Jordán, Manuel. 1996. Tossing Life in a Basket: Art and Divination among Chokwe, Lunda, Luvale and Related Peoples of Northwestern Zambia. Ph.D. diss., University of Iowa.

Jordán, Manuel, ed. 1998. *Art and Initiation among Chokwe and Related Peoples*. Munich: Prestel.

Katawola, H. M. 1965. *Ndangwishi jaValuvale*. Lusaka: Neczam.

Keane, Webb. 1998. Calvin in the Tropics: Objects and Subjects at the Religious Frontier. In *Border Fetishisms: Material Objects in Unstable Spaces*, edited by Patricia Spyer, 13-35. New York: Routledge.

Kingdon, Jonathan. 1997. *The Kingdon Field Guide to African Mammals*. San Diego: Academic Press.

Kirshenblatt-Gimblett, Barbara. 1989. Objects of Memory: Material Culture as Life Review. In *Folk Groups and Folklore Genres: A Reader*, edited by Elliott Oring, 329-38. Logan: Utah State University Press.

Kopytoff, Igor. 1981. Knowledge and Belief in Suku Thought. *Africa* 51 (3):96-110.

——. 1986. The Cultural Biography of Things: Commoditization as Process. In *The Social Life of Things: Commodities in Cultural Perspective*, edited by Arjun Appadurai, 64-95. Cambridge: Cambridge University Press.

Kramer, Fritz. 1993/1987. *The Red Fez: Art and Spirit Possession in Africa*. London: Verso.

La Fontaine, J. S. 1985. Person and Individual: Some Anthropological Reflections. In *The Category of the Person: Anthropology, Philosophy, History*, edited by Michael Carrithers, Steven Collins, and Steven Lukes, 123-40. Cambridge: Cambridge University Press.

Lakoff, George, and Mark Johnson. 1980. *Metaphors We Live By*. Chicago: University of Chicago Press.

Lambek, Michael. 1998. The Sakalava Poiesis of History: Realizing the Past through Spirit Possession in Madagascar. *American Ethnologist* 25 (2):106-27.

Leder, Drew. 1990. *The Absent Body*. Chicago: University of Chicago Press.

Lewis, I. M. 1971. *Ecstatic Religion: A Study of Shamanism and Spirit Possession*. London: Routledge.

Lienhardt, Godfrey. 1985. Self: Public, Private—Some African Representations. In *The Category of the Person: Anthropology, Philosophy, History*, edited by Michael Carrithers, Steven Collins, and Steven Lukes, 141-55. Cambridge: Cambridge University Press.

Lima, Mesquitela. 1971. *Les fonctions sociologiques des figurines de culte hamba dans la société et dans la culture tshokwe* (Angola). Luanda: Instituto de Investigação Científica de Angola.

Livingstone, David. 1857. *Missionary Travels and Researches in South Africa*. London: John Murray.

Lovejoy, Paul, ed. 1983. *Transformations in Slavery: A History of Slavery in Africa*. Cambridge: Cambridge University Press.

MacGaffey, Wyatt. 1977. Fetishism Revisited: Kongo Nkisi in Sociological Perspective. *Africa* 47:140-52.

———. 1988. Complexity, Astonishment and Power: The Visual Vocabulary of Kongo Minkisi. *Journal of Southern African Studies* 14 (2):188-203.

———. 1990. The Personhood of Ritual Objects: Kongo Minkisi. *Etnofoor* 3 (1):45-61.

———. 1993. The Eyes of Understanding: Kongo Minkisi. In *Astonishment and Power*, edited by Wyatt MacGaffey and M. D. Harris, 21-103. Washington, D.C.: Smithsonian Institution Press.

———. 1994. Notes and Comments: African Objects and the Idea of Fetish. *Res* 25:123-31.

———. 2000. *Kongo Political Culture: The Conceptual Challenge of the Particular*. Bloomington: Indiana University Press.

Mackworth-Praed, Cyril W., and Captain C. H. B. Grant. 1962. *Birds of the Southern Third of Africa*. London: Longman.

Malinowski, Bronislaw. 1948. Magic, Science and Religion. In *Magic, Science and Religion and Other Essays*. Boston: Beacon Press.

Marcum, J. 1969. *The Angolan Revolution*. 2 vols. Cambridge, Mass.: MIT Press.

Martins, João Vicente. 1993. *Crenças, adivinhação e medicina tradicionais dos tutchokwe do nordeste de Angola*. Lisbon: Instituto de Investigação Científica Tropical.

Marx, Karl. 1964. *Pre-capitalist Economic Formations*. Translated by J. Cohen. London: Lawrence and Wishart.

———. 1975. *Early Writings*. Translated by Rodney Livingstone and Gregor Benton. New York: Vintage.

Marx, Karl, and Frederick Engels. 1976. The German Ideology. Translated by C. Dutt. In *Karl Marx, Frederick Engels: Collected Works*, 5:19-608. Moscow: Progress Publishers.

Mauss, Marcel. 1968. L'art et le myth d'après M. Wundt. In *Oeuvres*, vol. 2. Paris: Minuit.

McCulloch, Merran. 1951. *The Southern Lunda and Related Peoples (Northern Rhodesia, Belgian Congo, Angola)*. London: International African Institute.

Messiant, Christine. 1998. Angola: The Challenge of Statehood. In *History of Central Africa: The Contemporary Years Since 1960*, edited by David Birmingham and Phyllis M. Martin, 131-66. London: Longman.

Miers, Suzanne, and Igor Kopytoff, eds. 1977. *Slavery in Africa: Historical and Anthropological Perspectives*. Madison: University of Wisconsin Press.

Mijere, Nsolo J., ed. 1995. *African Refugees and Human Rights in Host Countries: The Long-Term Demographic, Environmental, Economic, Social, and Psychological Impacts of Angolan Refugees in Zambia*. New York: Vantage Press.

Miller, Joseph C. 1970. Cokwe Trade and Conquest in the Nineteenth Century. In *Pre-Colonial African Trade: Essays on Trade in Central and Eastern Africa Before 1900*, edited by Richard Gray and David Birmingham, 175-201. London: Oxford University Press.

———. 1972. The Imbangala and the Chronology of Early Central African History. *Journal of African History* 13 (4):549-74.

———. 1981. Lineages, Ideology and the History of Slavery in Western Central Africa. In *Ideology of Slavery in Africa*, edited by Paul E. Lovejoy, 41-71. Beverly Hills, Calif.: Sage.

———. 1988. *The Way of Death: Merchant Capitalism and the Angolan Slave Trade 1730–1830*. Madison: University of Wisconsin Press.

Mitchell, J. Clyde. 1954. The Distribution of African Labour by Area of Origin on the Copper Mines of Northern Rhodesia. *Rhodes-Livingstone Journal* 14:30-36.

Newitt, Malyn. 2008. Angola in Historical Context. In *Angola: The Weight of History*, edited by Patrick Chabal and Nuno Vidal, 19-92. New York: Columbia University Press.

Orley, John. 1994. Psychological Disorders among Refugees: Some Clinical and Epidemiological Considerations. In *Amidst Peril and Pain: The Mental Health and Well-Being of the World's Refugees*, edited by Anthony J. Marsella, Thomas Bornemann, Solvig Ekblad, and John Orley, 193-206. Washington, D.C.: American Psychological Association.

Palmeirim, Manuela. 1998. The King's Crowns: Hierarchy in the Making among the Aruwund (Lunda). In *Art and Initiation among Chokwe and Related Peoples*, edited by Manuel Jordán, 21-28. Munich: Prestel.

Palmer, Eve, and Norah Pitman. 1972. *Trees of Southern Africa: Covering All the Indigenous Species in the Republic of South Africa, South-West Africa, Botswana, Lesotho & Swaziland*. 3 vols. Cape Town: A. A. Balkema.

Papstein, Robert J. 1978. The Upper Zambezi: A History of the Luvale People, 1000-1900. Ph.D. diss., University of California, Los Angeles.

———. 1989. From Ethnic Identity to Tribalism: The Upper Zambezi Region of Zambia, 1830-1981. In *The Creation of Tribalism in Southern Africa*, edited by Leroy Vail, 372-94. Berkeley: University of California Press.

Parker, Melissa. 1996. Social Devastation and Mental Health in Northeast Africa. In *In Search of Cool Ground: War, Flight, and Homecoming in Northeast Africa*, edited by Tim Allen, 262-73. Trenton, N.J.: Africa World Press.

Parkin, David. 1991. Simultaneity and Sequencing in the Oracular Speech of Kenyan Diviners. In *African Divination Systems: Ways of Knowing*, edited by Philip M. Peek, 173-91. Bloomington: Indiana University Press.

———. 1999. Mementoes as Transitional Objects in Human Displacement. *Journal of Material Culture* 4 (3):303-20.

Peek, Philip M. 1991a. African Divination Systems: Non-Normal Modes of Cognition. In *African Divination Systems: Ways of Knowing*, edited by Philip M. Peek, 193-212. Bloomington: Indiana University Press.

Peek, Philip M., ed. 1991b. *African Divination Systems: Ways of Knowing*. Bloomington: Indiana University Press, 1991.

Pélissier, René. 1974. Conséquences démographiques des révoltes en Afrique portugaise (1961-1970): Essai d'interpretation. *Révue Française d'Histoire d'Outre Mer* 61 (222):34-73.

Pels, Peter. 1998. The Spirit of Matter: On Fetish, Rarity, Fact, and Fancy. In *Border Fetishisms: Material Objects in Unstable Spaces*, edited by Patricia Spyer, 91-121. New York: Routledge.

Pemberton, John, III, ed. 2000. *Insight and Artistry in African Divination*. Washington, D.C.: Smithsonian Institution Press.

Pietz, William. 1985. The Problem of the Fetish, I. *Res* 9:5-17.

———. 1987. The Problem of the Fetish, II: The Origin of the Fetish. *Res* 13:23-47.

———. 1988. The Problem of the Fetish, III: Bosman's Guinea and the Enlightenment Theory of Fetishism. *Res* 16:103-23.

———. 1993. Fetishism and Materialism: The Limits of Theory in Marx. In *Fetishism as Cultural Discourse*, edited by Emily Apter and William Pietz, 119-51. Ithaca, N.Y.: Cornell University Press.

Poewe, Karla O. 1978a. Matriliny in the Throes of Change: Kinship, Descent and Marriage in Luapula, Zambia. Part One. *Africa* 48 (3):205-18.

———. 1978b. Matriliny in the Throes of Change: Kinship, Descent and Marriage in Luapula, Zambia. Part Two. *Africa* 48 (4):353-67.

———. 1978c. Religion, Matriliny, and Change: Jehovah's Witnesses and Seventh-Day Adventists in Luapula, Zambia. *American Ethnologist* 5 (2):303-21.

Powles, Julia. 2000. Road 65: A Narrative Ethnography of a Refugee Settlement in Zambia. Ph.D. diss., Oxford University.

Pritchett, James A. 2001. *The Lunda-Ndembu: Style, Change, and Social Transformation in South Central Africa*. Madison: University of Wisconsin Press.

Quinton, Anthony. 1967. Knowledge and Belief. In *The Encyclopedia of Philosophy*, edited by P. Edwards, 345-52. New York: Macmillan Free Press.

Redinha, José. 1948. Costumes religiosos e feiticistas dos kiokos de Angola. Paper presented at the Geographic Society of Lisbon.

———. 1953. *Campanha etnográfica ao Tchiboco (Alto-Tchicapa): Notas de viagem*. Vol. 1. Lisbon: Companhia de Diamantes de Angola.

———. 1958. *Etnosociologia do nordeste de Angola*. Lisbon: Agência Geral do Ultramar.

———. 1969. *O fenómeno económico e a etnografia (ensaio)*. Luanda: Centro de Informação e Turismo de Angola.

Reefe, Thomas Q. 1983. The Societies of the Eastern Savanna. In *History of Central Africa*, edited by D. Birmingham and P. M. Martin, 2:160-204. London: Longman.

Roberts, Mary Nooter. 2000. Proofs and Promises: Setting Meaning Before the Eyes. In *Insight and Artistry in African Divination*, edited by John Pemberton III, 63-82. Washington, D.C.: Smithsonian Institution Press.

Robertson-Smith, W. 1884. *Lectures on the Religion of the Semites*. London: Adam & Charles Black.

Rodrigues de Areia, Manuel L. 1978. Le panier divinatoire des tshokwe. *Arts d'Afrique Noire* 26:30-47.

———. 1985. *Les symboles divinatoires: Analyse socio-culturelle d'une technique de divination des Cokwe de l'Angola (ngombo ya cisuka)*. Coimbra, Portugal: Centro de Estudos Africanos, Universidade de Coimbra.

Rubin, Arnold. 1993. Accumulation: Power and Display in African Sculpture. In *Arts of Africa, Oceania, and the Americas: Selected Readings*, edited by Janet Catherine Berlo and Lee Anne Wilson, 4-21. Upper Saddle River, N.J.: Prentice Hall.

Ryle, Gilbert. 1949. Knowing How and Knowing That. In *The Concept of Mind*, 25-61. New York: Barnes & Noble.

Sakatengo, Jeremiah C. 1947. *Tribal Customs of the Lovale: Vilika vyaChisemwa cha-Valovale*. N.p.: Lovedale Press.

Sangambo, Mose Kaputungu. 1979. *The History of the Luvale People and Their Chieftainship*. Los Angeles: Africa Institute for Applied Research.

Schachtzabel, Alfred. 1923. *Im Hochland von Angola*. Dresden: Verlag Deutsche Buchwerkstätten.

Schapera, I. 1947. *Migrant Labour and Tribal Life*. Oxford: Oxford University Press.

Schindler, Norman. 1986. Fridolin Schindler of Luvaleland: The Story and Times of a Pioneer Missionary in the Angolan Hinterland. Typescript held by the Rhodes House Library, Oxford.

Shaw, Rosalind. 1985. Gender and the Structuring of Reality in Temne Divination: An Interactive Study. *Africa* 55 (3):286-303.

———. 1991. Splitting Truths from Darkness: Epistemological Aspects of Temne Divination. In *African Divination Systems: Ways of Knowing*, edited by Philip M. Peek, 137-52. Bloomington: Indiana University Press.

———. 2002. *Memories of the Slave Trade: Ritual and the Historical Imagination in Sierra Leone*. Chicago: University of Chicago Press.

Silva, Sónia. 1998. The Birth of a Divination Basket. In *Art and Initiation among Chokwe and Related Peoples*, edited by Manuel Jordán, 141-52. Munich: Prestel.

———. 1999. Vicarious Selves: Divination Baskets and Angolan Refugees in Zambia. Ph.D. diss., Indiana University, Bloomington.

———. 2003. *A vez dos cestos / Time for baskets*. Lisbon: Museu Nacional de Etnologia.

———. 2004. *Vidas em jogo: Cestas de adivinhação e refugiados angolanos na Zâmbia*. Lisbon: Instituto de Ciências Sociais.

———. 2009. Mothers of Solitude: Childlessness and Intersubjectivity in the Upper Zambezi. *Anthropology & Humanism* 34 (2):179-202.

Smith, William. 1744. *A New Voyage to Guinea*. London: Nourse.

Spring, Anita. 1976. Women's Rituals and Natality among the Luvale of Zambia. Ph.D. diss., Cornell University.

———. 1982. Women and Men as Refugees: Differential Assimilation of Angolans in Zambia. In *Involuntary Migration and Settlement*, edited by Art Hansen and A. Oliver-Smith, 37-47. Boulder, Colo.: Westview Press.

Spyer, Patricia. 1998. *Border Fetishisms: Material Objects in Unstable Spaces*. New York: Routledge.

Stoller, Paul. 1989a. *Fusion of the Worlds: An Ethnography of Possession among the Songhay of Niger*. Chicago: University of Chicago Press.

———. 1989b. *The Taste of Ethnographic Things: The Senses in Anthropology*. Philadelphia: University of Pennsylvania Press.

———. 1995. *Embodying Colonial Memories: Spirit Possession, Power, and the Hauka in West Africa*. New York: Routledge.

———. 1997. *Sensuous Scholarship*. Philadelphia: University of Pennsylvania Press.

Straus, Erwin. 1963. The Spectrum of the Senses. In *The Primary World of Senses: A Vindication of Sensory Experience*, 367-79. London: Collier-Macmillan.

Stroeken, Koen. 2004. In Search of the Real: The Healing Contingency of Sukuma Divination. In *Divination and Healing: Potent Visions*, edited by Michael Winkelman and Philip M. Peek, 29-55. Tucson: University of Arizona Press.

Tambiah, Stanley J. 1968. The Magical Power of Words. *Man* 3 (2):175-208 .

———. 1979. A Performative Approach to Ritual. *Proceedings of the British Academy* 65:113-69.

———. 1990. *Magic, Science, Religion, and the Scope of Rationality*. Cambridge: Cambridge University Press.

Tedlock, Barbara. 2001. Divination as a Way of Knowing: Embodiment, Visualization, Narrative, and Interpretation. *Folklore* 112:189-97.

———. 2006. Toward a Theory of Divinatory Practice. *Anthropology of Consciousness* 17 (2):62-77.

Tonkin, Elizabeth. 2004. Consulting Ku Jlople: Some Histories of Oracles in West Africa. *Journal of the Royal Anthropological Institute* 10:539-60.

Tucker, Leona S. 1940. The Divining Basket of the Ovimbundu. *Journal of the Royal Anthropological Institute of Great Britain and Ireland* 70:171-202.

Turner, Edith. 2004. Drumming, Divination, and Healing: The Community at Work. In *Divination and Healing: Potent Visions*, edited by Michael Winkelman and Philip M. Peek, 55-80. Tucson: University of Arizona Press.

Turner, Victor. 1957. *Schism and Continuity in an African Society: A Study of Ndembu Village Life*. Manchester: Manchester University Press.

———. 1967/1959. Muchona de Hornet, Interpreter of Religion. In *The Forest of Symbols: Aspects of Ndembu Ritual*, 131-50. Ithaca, N.Y.: Cornell University Press.

———. 1967/1965. Color Classification in Ndembu Ritual: A Problem in Primitive Classification. In *The Forest of Symbols: Aspects of Ndembu Ritual*, 59-92. Ithaca, N.Y.: Cornell University Press.

———. 1967. *The Forest of Symbols: Aspects of Ndembu Ritual*. Ithaca, N.Y.: Cornell University Press.

———. 1968. *The Drums of Affliction: A Study of Religious Processes among the Ndembu of Zambia*. Oxford: Clarendon Press for the International African Institute.

———. 1974. *Dramas, Fields, and Metaphors: Symbolic Action in Human Society*. Ithaca, N.Y.: Cornell University Press.

———. 1975/1961. Ndembu Divination: Its Symbolism and Techniques. In *Revelation and Divination in Ndembu Ritual*, 207-338. Ithaca, N.Y.: Cornell University Press.

———. 1975. *Revelation and Divination in Ndembu Ritual*. Ithaca, N.Y.: Cornell University Press.

———. 1982. *From Ritual to Theatre: The Human Seriousness of Play*. New York: PAJ Publications.

United Nations High Commissioner for Refugees (UNHCR). 1996. Report of the United Nations High Commissioner for Refugees, 1996. http://www.unhcr.org.

———. 2002. Africa Fact Sheet—June 2002. http://www.unhcr.org.

———. 2009. UNHCR Global Appeal 2010-2011—Zambia. http://www.unhcr.org.

U.S. Committee for Refugees (USCR). 1987. *Uprooted Angolans: From Crisis to Catastrophe*. Washington, D.C.: American Council for Nationalities Service.

———. 2002. *World Refugee Survey 2002*. Washington, D.C.: USCR.

van Binsbergen, Wim. 1987. Likota lya Bankoya: Memory, Myth and History. *Cahiers d'Études Africaines* 107-8: 359-92.

Vansina, Jan. 1966. *Kingdoms of the Savanna: A History of Central African States until European Occupation*. Madison: University of Wisconsin Press.

Vellut, Jean-Luc. 1972. Notes sur le Lunda et la frontière luso-africaine (1700–1900). *Études d'Histoire Africaine* 3:61-166.

Von Oppen, Achim. 1994. *Terms of Trade and Terms of Trust: The History and Contexts of Pre-Colonial Market Production Around the Upper Zambezi and Kasai*. Münster: Lit Verlag.

Wastiau, Boris. 2000. *Mahamba: The Transforming Arts of Spirit Possession among the Luvale-Speaking People*. Fribourg, Switzerland: Fribourg University Press.

Werbner, Richard. 1989. Tswapong Wisdom Divination: Making the Hidden Seen. In *Ritual Passage Sacred Journey: The Process and Organization of Religious Movement*. Washington, D.C.: Smithsonian Institution Press.

———. 1991. *Tears of the Dead: The Social Biography of an African Family*. Washington, D.C.: Smithsonian Institution Press.

White, Charles M. N. 1947. Divination among the Lunda and Lwena with Some Suggestions as to Modern Times. Typescript filed in sec2/990, National Archives of Zambia.

———. 1948a. Notes on Some Metaphysical Concepts of the Balovale Tribes. *African Studies* 7:146-56.

———. 1948b. The Supreme Being in the Beliefs of the Balovale Tribes. *African Studies* 7 (1):29-35.

———. 1948c. Witchcraft, Divination and Magic among the Balovale Tribes. *Africa* 18 (2):81-104.

———. 1949a. Stratification and Modern Changes in an Ancestral Cult. *Africa* 19 (4):324-31.

———. 1949b. The Balovale Peoples and Their Historical Background. *Rhodes-Livingstone Journal* 8:26-41.

———. 1957. Clan, Chieftainship, and Slavery in Luvale Political Organization. *Africa* 27 (1):59-75.

———. 1959. *A Preliminary Survey of Luvale Rural Economy.* Manchester: Manchester University Press.

———. 1960. *An Outline of Luvale Social and Political Organization.* Manchester: Manchester University Press.

———. 1961. *Elements of Luvale Beliefs and Rituals.* Manchester: Manchester University Press.

———. 1962. *Tradition and Change in Luvale Marriage.* Manchester: Manchester University Press.

White, C. M. N., and W. F. H. Ansell. 1966. A List of Luvale and Lunda Mammal Names. *The Puku* 4:181-85.

Whyte, Susan Reynolds. 1991. Knowledge and Power in Nyole Divination. In *African Divination Systems: Ways of Knowing,* edited by Philip M. Peek, 153-72. Bloomington: Indiana University Press.

———. 1997. *Questioning Misfortune: The Pragmatics of Uncertainty in Eastern Uganda.* Cambridge: Cambridge University Press.

Wilce, James M. 2001. Divining *Troubles,* or *Divining* Troubles? Emergent and Conflictual Dimensions of Bangladesh Divination. *Anthropological Quarterly* 74 (4):190-200.

Wilson, Ken. 1986. The Integration of Angolan Refugees in Western and North-Western Zambia. Ph.D. diss., University College London.

Winkelman, Michael, and Philip M. Peek. 2004. Introduction: Divination and Healing Processes. In *Divination and Healing: Potent Visions,* edited by Michael Winkelman and Philip M. Peek, 3-25. Tucson: University of Arizona Press.

Winkelman, Michael, and Philip M. Peek, eds. 2004. *Divination and Healing: Potent Visions.* Tucson: University of Arizona Press.

Young, Allan. 1977. Order, Analogy, and Efficacy in Ethiopian Medical Divination. *Culture, Medicine, and Psychiatry* 1 (2):183-99.

Zeitlyn, David. 2001. Finding Meaning in the Text: The Process of Interpretation in Text-Based Divination. *Journal of the Royal Anthropological Institute* 7:225-40.

Index

Page numbers in italics indicate images.

adulthood of the *lipele* (a basket divination séance), 83–122; aftermath, 120–21; arriving for the consultation, 88–89; basket divination and ancestral knowledge, 121–33; broken arrows, 89; choice of the diviner Mutondo, 85, *86*; Chuki's epilepsy, 83–85, 147n1; collecting the payment, 113–14; the consulter Chinyama and his son Chuki, 83–87; and death consultations, 89; the divination proper (*kutaha*), 94–119, 126–29; diviner's moments of reflexivity, 95; divining/diagnosing the cause of Chuki's illness, 99–110, 114–18, 119, 121–22; expression *Ngungu-e* to close the invocation, 94; initial invocation while shaking the *musambo* rattle, 90–94, *91*; the *jipelo* articles/configurations, 88, 95, *99*, *101–2*, *104*, *107–8*, *117*, 126–29; Mutondo's rebuke of Chinyama, 87, 105; performative style of the divination proper, 94–95; slavery accusation, 103–6, 114–18; therapeutic procedure to remove the *ponde* affliction, 118, 122; uncovering the *lipele* and tracing the white and red lines, 89–90; white kaolin clay to be rubbed on the chest, 119–20; witchcraft fears, 85, 123. *See also* knowledge

agency, 45, 82. *See also* ritual

ancestral knowledge: basket divination and, 121–33; commoditization and, 82, 137

André, Carl, 134

Angolan refugees, 9–14, 17; Chavuma (the 1990s), 9–13, 25, 45–46, 143n8; clans and, 25, 144n6; influxes of, 9–10; and invocation of political leaders during divination séance, 90, 92; official refugee settlements, 10, 11, 121; ritual attendance and, 58, 65; silence and, 11–14, 22–25, 29, 54, 82–83; suffering in exile, 10, 29, 46, 84, 140; villages of recent settlers, 25; witchcraft and, 80; work and lucrative activities, 45–46

Angolan wars, 10, 64, 82–83, 121; colonial rule and liberation movements of the 1960s, 9–10, 23; the FNLA, 10; independent Angola, 10, 23; *jipelo* articles and, 13, 143n10; Lusaka Peace Accord, 83; MPLA, 9–10, 23, 64, 90; UNITA, 9–10, 23, 83, 90, 121

anthropomorphization, 15–16, 17

Appadurai, Arjun: commoditization theory, 4–5, 16–17, 24–25, 34, 46–47, 135–38, 148n2; "ex-commodities," 4, 135–37; "methodological fetishism," 17

Arendt, Hannah, 42

Armstrong, Robert, 134

art, 42, 134; African, 3, 8, 134, 135–36

basket divination in northwest Zambia: bodily experience and the divinatory journey, 128–29; clarity and, 126–29; during colonialism, 12–13; cultural continuity and, 13–14, 92; as cultural practice, 9, 17, 140; divinatory symbolism/ritual symbolism, 123; embodied and propositional knowledge and, 8, 123–26, 133; origins of *lipele* divination, 48–52, 138–39; personification, objectification, de-objectification, 5–6, 16–17, 140–41; social redress/jurisprudence and, 130–32; speech and discourse in, 127–29; three facets, 6–9; as way of doing (ritual efficacy), 6–7, 17, 76–81, 86–88, 126–29, 141; as way of knowing, 7– 9, 17, 82, 121–33, 141; as way of making a living, 8–9, 17, 42–46, 132, 139–41; as work and labor, 37–47, 137–41. *See also jipelo* articles and *jipelo* configurations; *lipele* (divination basket)

Acknowledgments

This book draws on fieldwork I conducted in Chavuma, northwest Zambia, mostly between May 1995 and December 1996. I thank the Wenner-Gren Foundation and Calouste Gulbenkian Foundation for their financial support. I conducted two months of preliminary research in 1994 thanks to the Indiana University David C. Skomp Fund. I had the opportunity to return to Zambia for additional periods of three months in 1999 and two months in 2002, this time with support from the Smithsonian Institution and the Fundação para a Ciência e Tecnologia, respectively.

Over time, I have accumulated many debts of gratitude. I thank all the individuals mentioned in this book, especially diviners Samafunda, Sanjamba, Sakutemba, Sangombe, and Mutondo, basket maker Pezo and her husband Ndonji, fisherman Kakoma and his daughter Alice, and Sapasa and his nephew Chinyama. I am indebted to my hosts Rose Chikunga, Harrison Chikunga, and Sapasa; my research assistants Roy Mbundu, Cedric Chikunga, and Henry Sawendele; the late *manduna* Maseka and Mutonga; the missionaries stationed in Chavuma; the Baptista brothers and their friend Lopes; and Joerg Mellentluh. For my preliminary research, conducted mostly in Kabompo, I owe much to Manuel Jordán, Ben and Kutemba Robertson, Makina's family, and Ilse Mwanza.

I am equally indebted to Paula Girshick, Michael Jackson, Phyllis Martin, Richard Bauman, the anonymous reviewers of my book manuscript, my editor Peter Agree, and the production team of Penn Press. Their sharp comments, insightful ideas, and encouragement influenced this book in countless ways. I am also grateful to Sean D'Angelo, Julia Powles, Anna Stroulia, and Boris Wastiau for their friendship and support, and to Keith, Kameshi, and Chisola, who were always there.